MEMORIES OF
MAX

A Father's Story

Allan Buchanan

a fellow "Sam"
at Bracknell
Known as "Will"

This book is dedicated to childhood cancer survivors and to those who fell by the wayside.

To Max, who showed me the strength and love I had within, and how easily these can be lost, and to Paula, who helped me find them again.

CONTENTS

Preface

This is a father's story about my son Max, and it outlines my hopes and fears, before, during, and beyond his cancers. It portrays the love that developed between us both and my pain following his death. I describe the emotions experienced by the parent of a cancer-stricken child, which include the hills and mountains climbed, and the crevasses and valleys you fall into on this journey.

This book includes fragments, snapshots, and indelible stains left with me after Max died, but it does not and could never fully portray what happened to us as a family. I culled the content from a diary written on and off throughout his second illness. It is far longer than the book, and a raw disturbing journal of the darkest moments in my life.

The book's message is one of hope and shows the amazing courage and fortitude displayed by children undergoing cancer treatment. It highlights from a father's perspective the possibility of surviving those dark places, and even on the blackest of nights; a light can shine.

Max emerged as a distant and damaged shell after his leukaemia, but over the next two years gained strength to become a healthy child again. The second diagnosis, this time for a tumour, resulted in him struggling to cope and becoming angry and depressed. I and my wife, Sara, realised we could not help him medically. However, we could teach him the skills needed to fight his illness and improve his quality of life during treatment. Max rewarded us with a fierce determination and willpower as he developed the confidence and independence required to overcome his disabilities. Like many children with cancer, he adapted and lived life as fully as possible.

I have changed every name in the book, except Max's, to shield individuals because of the personal aspects of the narrative.

Allan Buchanan – November 1999.

Admission

Chapter 1

t started strangely, with an unexpected event and a sad precursor to our own story. The episode involved our next-door neighbour, a gay man in his fifties and a colourful eccentric. Although initially a good acquaintance, we fell out after he became vindictive and rude to Sara. She phoned me at work on Thursday the 22nd July 1993 and elatedly described how a bailiff had visited to reclaim our neighbour's mortgage. In a later call, she sombrely told me the police were investigating his suicide after discovering him hanging from the stairwell rafters. His death shocked us. Our nemesis began the next day.

Sara rang me at work during the following afternoon and said our four-year-old son Max was unwell. He had complained of a headache and tottered while playing outside with his best friend. I left and walked the half mile back to our house to help her. Max had a high temperature, which was not too worrying, but his staggering alarmed me. He had recently started school and kept coming home with purple bruises on his legs. When asked whether other children were bullying him, he said the marks resulted from enjoyable rough and tumble play. At no point did we relate his contusions with the symptoms seen in the garden.

Max had a fever when I checked on him at eight o'clock the next morning. I phoned the on-call doctor, who arrived three hours later, but despite his concern was unwilling to make a specific diagnosis. He instructed me to take Max to the local hospital straightaway with a sealed note for the examining physician.

After a brief wait in reception, a nurse took us to an examination room. Max's condition continued deteriorating, and twenty minutes afterwards she took his blood pressure and samples of blood and urine. A doctor arrived to question the staff but was irritated by the interruption of her lunch break, and this hostility was annoying and struck me as being unnecessary. Her irritation soon changed to extreme concern after hearing Max's details, and I realised the gravity of his illness as she barked orders to the nurses.

My unease grew because despite still being conscious, Max was sinking rapidly and had passed from being unwell to ill. I reined in my worries and remained positive as the health professionals addressed his symptoms. Six nurses piled into the tiny room and the doctor turned and spoke to me.

"Mister Buchanan, please wait outside while we do the next test," she said curtly.

"Sorry, but I'm not leaving Max. What are you going to do?"

"We have to give your son an urgent lumbar puncture and cannot use anaesthetic because of time constraints. These nurses need to hold him still during the procedure, and there's not enough space for you in here. On other occasions parents have fainted or become hysterical, so please can you wait outside for a few minutes? It won't take long."

Max whispered feebly, "Dad, don't go."

This moment marked the point where my world began to disintegrate, though I was unaware of it at the time.

"Sorry, but I have no intention of leaving my son because he needs me by his side. I won't become agitated."

Intense discussion ensued between the doctor and nurses.

"Okay, you can stay, but you must crouch down next to him."

The room measured eight feet by ten, confirming her concerns regarding the lack of space. Max lay on a children's examination bed surrounded by the staff, and I squatted on the floor to the left of his head. Three nurses stood alongside me, one at the end, and two beside the doctor on Max's right side. Their aim was to sample cerebrospinal fluid to aid his diagnosis. The surrounding medics alarmed him, so I held his hand, proffered soothing words, and said the test would not take long. The doctor tried the spinal tap twice and became more agitated after each failure, but she succeeded on the third attempt. On each occasion Max suffered pain despite his semi-conscious state, and he clenched my hand with a fierce grip as his body arched and he screamed in agony. As predicted by the doctor, watching Max's pain left me deeply distressed.

Max's anxiety abated after the spinal tap because his worsening condition prevented further complaint. The nurses administered various drugs and attached monitoring equipment and intravenous drips. They then moved him to a room, where he drifted into unconsciousness as I lay on a camp bed next to him. I still upheld my faith that the hospital would soon resolve his fever before we returned home in a few days.

A nurse wearing a facemask popped in to assess Max's condition and I asked her to watch him while I went to the toilet before phoning Sara with an update.

"Mister Buchanan, I'm sorry but we can't let you leave the room."

"Why not, what's wrong?"

"It's unclear whether Max's illness is infectious, so you must stay here until we have more information. If you need the lavatory, use the adjoining one through that door, and please make sure you wash your hands afterwards."

"Do you know what type of infection?"

"The doctor is unsure at the moment."

"How serious is this? Will I be off work for long?"

"We don't know yet but will update you when we have further information."

She left.

I became more realistic and recognised the potential seriousness of Max's illness, but concern about my potential absence from work showed that its true nature had still not dawned on me. My confidence sank as I reflected on the urgency of the lumbar puncture and the nurse's subsequent facemask. Meningitis was the only infection that I knew could strike a child so suddenly, and if this was the cause, were Sara or I infected? Pushing these pessimistic and reckless thoughts to the back of my mind, I realised I needed to wait for more information.

Later, a friend put her head round the door and asked after Max. I told her to stay outside due to the risk of infection and explained that we were waiting for a diagnosis. A nurse ushered her away. Nurses came and went but always answered my questions by saying that they still had no confirmation of Max's illness. This lack of knowledge alarmed me because I knew immediate treatment was imperative for meningitis. Did the doctors know what they were doing?

Sara arrived at the ward at six thirty that evening, and my refusal to allow her into the room caused momentary confusion. We questioned the attending nurse, who was unaware of any infection risks and allowed her to enter. No one had explained why there was no longer an issue, and I worried that either the wrong or no communication was passing between the changing nursing shifts. An alternative and darker implication was the withholding of new information. Max lay unconscious next to us as we sat and discussed potential causes for the illness and pondered his fate.

An hour later, while Sara watched over Max, I went to the Ward Reception Desk and queried whether there were any updates on his diagnosis. The doctor who had given the lumbar puncture apologised for the problems during the procedure. She confirmed that my former speculation of meningitis had also been her primary concern and the reason for the brief treatment time available. I appreciated her apology and asked if this infection had caused his illness. She replied that this was not the case, but that his blood test had highlighted a lower than expected number of white cells. Alarm bells rang inside my head, but then subsided because I could not remember the significance of this symptom.

A nurse summoned Sara and me for a discussion with the consultant at eight o'clock that evening. Despite Sara's apprehension, I still thought Max's illness was serious but not insurmountable. Two nurses took us to the meeting, and their presence puzzled me, but otherwise I was confident my son would soon receive treatment and recover. Our consultant, Dr Solomon, explained how the hospital was keeping the symptoms in check before arranging further therapy.

"Max is seriously ill, and I need to discuss his condition. You must listen very carefully to what I say, which may not make sense now, but you'll realise afterwards why I am structuring my discussion in this way. We first thought he had contracted meningitis, hence the lack of anaesthetic during the lumbar puncture. Our tests proved negative but highlighted a low white cell count, which raised suspicions and required further investigation. I'm sorry we've taken so long to get back to you, but we needed to be sure of our diagnosis, which we confirmed with later analysis."

"Max has septicaemia, another name for blood poisoning, and a scratch on his arm has resulted in a general infection throughout his body. We're giving him a transfusion and antibiotics to stabilise his condition. I've reserved a bed at one of the best hospitals in the country for his treatment, and he'll go there tomorrow. Do you both understand what I've said so far?"

Dr Solomon spoke with consideration, ensuring we absorbed as much information as possible. It blunted my optimism, and I realised Max's illness had progressed from serious to critical. This account hinted at fearsome scenarios, but he had not explained the root cause of the symptoms, which left me feeling confused. Sara pre-empted my prospective barrage of questions with a quiver in her voice.

"Are you telling us that Max has leukaemia?"

"Yes, I'm very sorry; we have diagnosed your son with leukaemia."

I reeled at this freight train of a statement. It was a hammer the size of a house with me as the anvil, and the end of my existence as I knew it. A tidal wave rears up, so tall you cannot see its crest, and a great chasm opens beneath you, dangerously beckoning. You try to resist and defy your senses, but its reality is undeniable. Into it slides your wife, your daughter, your career, your hopes and aspirations, and everything you have ever worked for and believed in. Your life slips into this vast gaping hole in the space of a couple of seconds that stretch out like an eternity. Your dear beloved son plunges into the abyss before anything else and there is nothing you can do; no get-out clause, no parachute, no escape. No one can prepare for this; it is incomprehensible.

While contemplating my life a year before this diagnosis, I was glad we had children, especially because we were lucky enough to have both a boy and girl. I worked in a well-paid job I enjoyed and found challenging and rewarding. Our lives had now taken an abrupt change of direction, and we had major problems. All the good and bad in my life disappeared into the black hole.

Distraught, Sara and I had a barrage of questions for Dr Solomon. What were Max's chances of survival? How did this happen? I had not realised the vast advances made in leukaemia treatment since my youth and assumed Max's diagnosis was a death sentence. The consultant assuaged my concern by telling us the illness was treatable, but he could not respond to our queries because of his unfamiliarity with the current therapies. The success rate between the two primary types of the disease differed, with one much higher than the other. He could not clarify the subtype, because this required specialised tests at the next hospital. The medical staff left after the consultation ended, and we phoned our respective parents. Afterwards we held on to each other and cried in turn and together as we acknowledged the traumatic news.

Sara returned home to look after our daughter Paula, while I stayed with Max. During the evening I asked Dr Solomon whether I needed to watch for changes in Max's condition or responses by the monitoring equipment. He said the nurses would visit our room regularly, but I should not hesitate in alerting them if I had any concerns. I queried how the septicaemia affected Max's leukaemia. He explained that they were treating the infection, and Max would travel to the Royal Marsden Hospital by ambulance the following morning if he got through the night.

"What do you mean 'if he gets through the night?'"

"Max's condition is critical and if we can't manage it, then he may not survive."

I was stunned by this first of many tremors after the earthquake.

"What are the chances you'll get it under control?"

"That depends on the degree of the infection and the extent Max's immune system can fight the septicaemia. We'll know within the next few hours how he's reacting to treatment, but I can't at present give you any fair assessment."

After thanking him for his frankness, I sat awake watching my poor unconscious child connected to his monitoring equipment. At two o'clock in the morning a doctor informed me that Max was responding to the antibiotics, and I slipped into a troubled slumber.

Confused and upset, I found myself in a cramped room full of medical apparatus, and my son lay next to me and close to dying. This was too much to comprehend, so I pinched my arm and to my surprise found myself in my bedroom at home. The whole incident had just been a traumatic dream, and its content and intensity were disturbing. My relief was palpable as I sat on the edge of my bed sweating, perplexed by Max's leukaemia, and trying to make sense of this distressing scenario. After reflecting for two minutes, I noticed the walls were fading. Frightened, I wondered if I was having a breakdown and then awoke from this unpleasant nightmare. Sara and I often experienced similar dreams and cruel mind deception during later perilous stages of Max's treatment.

I remember as a teenager discussing with a friend whether we would manage extreme scenarios in our future lives. Would we fight in a war, be brave, and survive the horrors? We were unsure, but then discussed the worst that could happen to you as a civilian. Our conclusion was the diagnosis of your child with leukaemia. How would we cope? Again, we did not know.

Life can be cruelly ironic.

The Unit

Chapter 2

The following morning Sara came back to the local hospital, and an ambulance took her and Max to the Royal Marsden. Founded in 1851, this was the first hospital in the world dedicated to cancer, and it has a renowned global reputation for quality of treatment and research. It includes two London hospitals, one based in Chelsea and the other in Sutton. The latter has the specialist wards reserved for the complex management of rare childhood cancers, and fortunately for us was only ten miles away from our house.

After spending the night watching over Max, I returned home to have a bath, get clothes, and prepare for the unknown. Afterwards I drove to the Children's Unit still tired and numb from the preceding tribulations.

On reaching the hospital, the signposting hinting at mysterious treatments and conditions alarmed me as I walked through the corridors, which were institutional, drab, and boring. How would this reality fit into our daily existence? How long could Max survive, and would I become an expert in the forthcoming weeks given my lack of any relevant knowledge about cancer treatment? I arrived at my destination, signified by a colourful painted picture of a jungle, wild animals, and the ominous words; "The Wolfson Children's Cancer Unit."

After entering an open foyer, I pressed a buzzer to let the staff know I had arrived but received no response. A few minutes later a nurse remotely opened the electronic lock, and I walked into the Unit full of apprehension.

Sunlight bathed the hallway and startled me, as did the colourful curtains and pictures lining the walls, which were in stark contrast to the former passageways. Unsure of what to expect, the stillness reminded me of a morgue and the eerie quietness was disturbing. The silence was unusual and caused by the prevailing lack of so few inpatients, but this does not happen often. If all the beds are in use, then outreach hospitals treat the children to cope with this lack of resources.

A nurse took me to Max's ward, and he managed a weak smile as I entered the room. Although looking washed out, he was sitting up in bed, which was a huge step forward from the previous evening at the local hospital. He paraded the intravenous line in his arm and told me how brave he had been, despite his crying during its painful insertion. Sara and I had many questions for the nurses, but they could not answer most of them until detailed testing divulged the exact nature of Max's cancer. They showed us round and inaugurated us into the daily procedures, but we were numb and absorbed little information in those first days.

The Unit had two wings, called the Outpatient and McElwain Wards, which were connected by double doors only accessed by staff.

The Outpatient Ward was used by nurses during the day to give children medication or tests before their return home. It included a sizeable waiting room and playing space linked to a treatment area. This contained three beds, and nurses examined patients or dispensed medicine here. Separate adjoining rooms were used for private chats between parents and nurses, or for treating children.

The McElwain Ward housed inpatients receiving life-threatening treatment. It was composed of several isolation rooms, together with three small wards that had the capacity to treat up to sixteen children. A cupboard beside each child's bed held another pull-down bed that enabled a parent to care for their child during the night.

When not bedbound, children play in the Unit corridors or use a large playroom and schoolroom staffed by trained Carers and schoolteachers. If they are receiving medication through drips, then they wheel the portable equipment and tubes along behind them.

Two rooms in the McElwain Ward were allocated to respective parents and adolescents for respite from the rest of the Unit. Rules forbade admittance to these rooms by younger patients.

A well-resourced kitchen enabled parents to cook meals for themselves, or for their offspring after refusal of hospital food. The Staff Room and Dispensary were the sole province of the doctors and nurses, as were the two small consulting rooms used for private conversations. Outside was a playground with a climbing frame and other equipment, but poor health prevented their use by most children.

Separate accommodation attached to the McElwain Ward held a kitchen, lounge, and bedrooms, allowing a second parent to stay overnight. The hospital reserved these rooms for the more serious cases, and we used them for a few weeks after our arrival.

After several days of tests, the doctors diagnosed Max with Acute Myeloid Leukaemia (AML), the subtype having a lower chance of survival. His condition deteriorated, so Sara and I wanted to dedicate our time to caring for him. The prospect of treatment was daunting, but we had to consider Paula's care before moving our lives to the hospital. A neighbour offered to look after her, and we accepted this suggestion with thanks, though did not realise that our absence would create later repercussions. I handed in my notice to my employer, a major American software company, but they told me I could go on indefinite sick leave, and that resignation was unnecessary. This enabled me to dedicate my time to Max's care.

During our first few days in one of the wards, I watched a father talking to his son, who was quiet and feeling low. The father climbed on to the bed, gave his child a hug and said how much he loved him. They embraced for a while, and the boy responded to the affection with rising spirits as the dad continued to talk softly. Most of this conversation was audible and a public display of private emotions. I was close to Max, though never showed my feelings this openly. But I had not been there long, and I too soon enacted those special family moments regardless of those present. You cease to care because the only thing that matters is your child's welfare.

We moved to an isolation room at the end of our first week because of Max's prevailing condition and an infection in the wards. Thankful for the privacy, we did not realise the disadvantages caused by our segregation. The lack of direct contact with other families meant it took us far longer to adjust to living in the Unit.

The Children's Cancer Unit has a dynamic of its own that works, but on a level having no bearing to the outside world. It consisted of a close-knit and supportive community throughout our time there. Each parent had one thing in common, irrespective of race, religion, class, creed, or colour; their child had cancer. Families mix with people they would never have normally met but who often became good friends.

Life varied between cheeriness and boredom, interspersed with routine tasks and the grim determination to get past the crisis of the moment. We were cheerful after progress during treatment, or when Max's morale improved. Tedium arose when his health was stable for a few days and nothing untoward happened. This is all relative. Despair was often the predominant emotion due to his potent chemotherapy and its dire complications.

The Unit has a camaraderie and closeness absent within the outside world. This breeds the familiarity occurring in a war, and in its peculiar way; this is a war. Each family has its individual horrific stories to tell, and yours is not special because another is always in a similar or worse state. You fight your own battles and those of others. Not only do you live with the difficulties of your child's illness, but also with the struggles of other children combating their disease. This may sound harsh but is the price paid for the mutual support provided. Parents comfort each other, laugh, and sometimes cry together because they are all in the same boat. You have an empathy with those families no one else can ever have, but your comprehension is partial because of widely differing circumstances.

Living in a Children's Cancer Unit is very abnormal compared to everyday life, and events are frequently radical and drastic, but often do not appear so at the time. There was more laughter and fewer tears than one would have expected, which can appear strange to an outsider. Every parent's circumstance is desperate, and they have little time for self-pity. Most get by because we have a stockpile of resilience deep inside, enabling us to survive in circumstances that suggest otherwise. This rarely summoned inner strength requires minimal conscious effort. We reserve it for life's emergencies, such as wars, concentration camps, and other horrors inflicted by humanity. This fortitude keeps the mind together and is not a rare gleaming jewel, but the power of very ordinary people. Sara and I witnessed it daily with the surrounding families and children in the Unit.

Parents cope to the best of their ability, which often exceeds any expectations or predictions made before the illness. They survive because they must, and those who are managing help others who have problems coping. Those supplying support know they may need similar care in the time ahead or have received the same comfort in the past.

After Max's admission to the Unit, the nurses warned Sara and I that our morale would rise and fall with the progress of his treatment and emotional state. The first you expect, but the second is disarming. We had a good day if he woke up cheerful, but if he awoke depressed, then we often sank to that level. These reactions have no relation to the therapy, but dissociating yourself from them becomes impossible. Like many other parents, we had difficulty judging our own emotions and realised the disease was a parasite that had taken control over our lives and enslaved us. When things are steady some normalcy appears, but you are aware this is an illusion.

Sara and I experienced occasions where the outward strength we showed to the world crumbled in the face of minor events. This is common and many in the Unit believed they were coping well, but also fell apart after a trivial mishap. Those that undid us were unpredictable and in normal cases just formed part of a trying day. We were unprepared for the venting of these stored stresses we had held at bay. In my case, this occurred when our car battery failed while my parents came to see Max at the hospital. The reorganisation of transport to get everyone back home left me stressed. I started running a bath on our return, but the hot tap sheared off in my hand. Tired and exhausted, I turned off the water supply and spent the remainder of the evening with the repairs. Despite my anxiety, this was nothing compared to the burdens we had endured over the preceding months.

The first occasion Sara experienced a minor misfortune that triggered significant reactions was the failure by a shop to mend her camera. Furious, because we wanted to photograph Max on his fifth birthday, she demanded an explanation but broke down in tears at their bumbling excuses and utter inefficiency. On her return she commented to me that coping with major problems was just about possible, but sometimes the trivial things pushed you beyond your limits. I agreed.

Another case occurred when Sara picked Paula up from school. Sara told a mother the cost of the damage from reversing into our car a week earlier. The ensuing hostility and shouting left Sara traumatised, and a teacher took her into the school shaking and unable to speak. Having no objective judgement of your emotional state is disturbing, leaving you suspicious of whether feelings are genuine or just surface reactions.

Max's health seesawed and after a few weeks we moved from the isolation room back into the wards. During both of Max's treatments, we spent time in every one of them. The return to the wards enabled us to mix with the other families. We lived in the Unit for over three and a half months and often formed a close friendship with a family, who then went home before returning weeks later. They always assumed it was a coincidence we were together again but were surprised when we said we had never left.

My observations of the behaviour of our own and other families during our time at the Unit resulted in me dividing childhood cancer into categories. They are set apart from each other based on the struggle of explaining your plight to anybody on a lower level. Each category reflects the effects of illness on the family concerned.

Class One in my taxonomy is the diagnosis and treatment of a first cancer. One can often discern the First Timers because many parents resemble comatose zombies during the first few days, especially when the news is a cruel thunderbolt out of the blue. These parents had lived their lives with their own hopes and goals. They dreamt of having another child, a better job, or of recovering from life's aberrations and everything thrown at them as it runs its course. These mothers and fathers placed their common aspirations on hold as they tried coming to terms with the devastation caused by their child's cancer. I found my early days in the Unit difficult because I resented the laughter and could not understand how parents could joke while their child lay critically ill in bed. How could they behave normally? It upset me, but I later understood some semblance of normality was necessary to survive under these conditions.

Parents can contribute hugely to their child's care while in the Unit. Reactions to chemotherapy resulted in Max spewing several times a day during his worst treatment. Although messy, you soon became used to cleaning and replacing the bedclothes. We measured his liquid intake and urine volume because keeping a balance is crucial. The side effects of the drugs, such as vomiting or diarrhoea, can lead to dehydration and also be life-threatening without replacement of lost fluid. This monitoring could be a challenging task if Max was not thirsty. We also took his potty to the sluice room to enable the nurses to examine his stools, which they checked for consistency, traces of blood, or other indications of complications. If he had a fever, then a laboratory analysed samples for an infection.

Childhood cancer patients require a Hickman Line, which enables nurses to infuse chemotherapy and drips, or inject drugs and withdraw blood samples. Three tubes join to form the central venous catheter, which goes through the chest, beneath the skin and up to the shoulder, before joining the jugular vein and accessing the heart. The gauze plaster sealing the entry point on the skin must remain sterile because infections can be fatal for an immunosuppressed child.

The nurses flushed Max's Hickman Line regularly to keep pathogens at bay when we were in the hospital, but at home I performed this task. It always caused me consternation because I had twice seen Max sinking towards coma after a line infection.

The children and nurses in the Unit called the Hickman Lines "Wigglies." Hospital volunteers stitch together coloured fabrics to create "Wiggly Bags", which hang round the neck and prevent the tubes from moving around under the child's clothing. Hickman Lines are a godsend in childhood cancer treatment because the alternative is a temporary tube inserted into a vein in the arm. It is unwieldy and used before introducing the line, but caused Max concern and often pain, and he dreaded them on the few occasions they were necessary. Another option is the use of a hypodermic needle, but this is harrowing for a child.

Sara and I lapsed into an insidious feature of Unit life after Max's admission. It occurs when parents focus on the child's wellbeing and pay scant regard to their own needs. We tried doing as much as possible and more for him, but this can lead to a damaging downward spiral. Worry and disturbances during the night lead to a lack of sleep. Tiredness and anxiety result in forgetting meals or missing them because you do not feel hungry, resulting in you not looking after yourself properly. The physical and mental stress grind you down, leading to less sleep as the process repeats itself. This feedback does not take long to intensify and continue unabated, and it pulls you downhill fast. Learning from our mistakes, we later avoided this pitfall by spending alternate days and nights supporting Max.

During Class One of my arbitrary classification, I became aware of Class Two: relapse, the reoccurrence of cancer. This is the sandman lurking in parents' nightmares, the ogre that follows you by day and disturbs your sleep at night. This setback signifies a substantial worsening of your child's chances of survival, because it is much harder to purge the disease if the chemotherapy failed the first time around.

Relapse is the Damoclean sword hanging over your child, interminable and held by such a thin thread. You cannot tell if or when it will fall or understand the consequences, but you know they will be dire. During the first cancer you meet parents and their relapsed children and wonder how they can go through this pain again. And again. And again. Coping with your child's disease draws on all your reserves and having enough strength a second time round seems inconceivable, yet you have seen many families do just that. I always felt a sickening emptiness on hearing about a new relapse; sometimes a patient in the Unit, occasionally friends of friends. You pray for them all.

I met a boy with a brain tumour who had relapsed nine times over five years. Although his sarcoma had not previously spread, it kept reactivating like a demented alarm clock. I often talked with him and eventually met his mum, who informed me they were awaiting his latest prognosis. The consultant delivered the outcome to the boy's parents next to their curtained bed, and he told them further treatment could not impede the disease. They were distraught after his departure.

The following day I asked the mother how she felt because her suffering needed acknowledgement. Even in the Unit people sometimes use the shunning defence of denial because the reality of other's sorrow is too much to bear. By saying something, however difficult and ineffectual, I was showing I cared. She told me their story, and this family had been through appalling torment over the years. What an earth can you say? I just listened to this distressed woman, because I had no effective words to relieve her anguish.

Between the end of Max's leukaemia treatment and the onset of his second cancer, I thought long and hard about the possibility of his relapse. These thoughts were not constant but occurred when I was not doing anything specific, and they filled me with dread. The prospect of his potential death crowded those contemplations and invaded the spare moments available to reflect on life. These ruminations were quiet yet relentless. Only after Max died did I realise how much pressure they exerted, and how they changed my outlook on the world.

As parents of a relapsed child, we faced the ordeal of meeting families we had known in the hospital during Max's leukaemia treatment. This led to the strange paradox of being glad to see them, but despondent because of our mutual and desperate circumstances. Old friends often greeted us, "Hi, how are you? In here for a check-up?" Sara and I shook our heads as Max and the other children chatted or played, forcing us adults to be careful about discussing the implications of his relapse. The conversation was just a stream of words, and the faces of these mothers and fathers betrayed their thoughts and unspoken horror. "Oh Christ, he's relapsed. Why? Please never let that happen to us."

Similar unexpected problems occurred when I tried helping families through their ordeal, because I had to report our own setback. A colleague at work posted an appeal for the Children's Unit after his child's leukaemia diagnosis. The news distressed me and so I donated to the fund, and afterwards rang the family to offer support and discuss my closeness to their circumstances. On meeting them weeks later at the hospital, explaining Max's subsequent relapse with a different cancer was very difficult and caused much confusion.

I wrote to a friend's family for a year because I wanted to help them come to terms with their child's leukaemia. Like us, they too had the same questions and foreboding thoughts. My letters tried to give honest and supportive answers to let them realise they were not alone in their worries. I did not know how to inform them of our tragic news because I had been as positive as possible, but Max's relapse had proved me wrong. How could I destroy whatever hope I might have provided? I did not contact them but received a caring letter back after they heard about our shocking update.

Class Three is the manifestation of a new and different cancer. Consultants warn you during the initial diagnosis that in exceptional circumstances the therapy can lead to another unrelated malignancy. Childhood cancers are scarce, and the existence of the illness is numbing as you prepare for the long haul of forthcoming treatment. Rare amongst the rare is incomprehensible and so you push it into the background and think "No, that'll never happen to us." Parents do not consider a different cancer as likely because they have more immediate concerns and this category does not linger within conscious thought. Throughout our stints at the hospital, I was only aware of a solitary family in Class Three; my own.

Class Four in my sad categorisation is a child's death. As newcomers, we heard little talk by anybody about children who had passed away. Everyone showed a sensitivity towards the families of the newly diagnosed, because the one thing uppermost in everyone's minds is "Will my child survive?" As we integrated more into the Unit, we became aware of past fatalities and those occurring while we were there. The staff try shielding mothers and fathers from the news of a recent loss, but it spreads like gossip on the school grapevine. Crushing, it affects parents and staff alike, and a quiet emptiness pervades the Unit. Updates about home deaths likewise soon pass to friends and circulate amongst others. This news devastates everybody and is the reminder of the perils facing all these families.

Everyone lived daily with the awareness of death within the life cycle of cancer-stricken children. I had always regarded this as the ultimate worst-case scenario, but later realised my ignorance. Class Five is the last and incomprehensible stage, as Death's cruel ratchet turns once more, resulting in the further death of a sibling, wife, or husband. Having lost my son, I cannot fathom this category or conceive how you contend with a further bereavement. I know a handful of families who suffered the loss of a parent or another child. It is extremely sobering to see your worst nightmares realised in another family while contemplating the next potential stage in your child's illness. There is always the realisation that these outcomes could so easily be your own.

I often saw baffling conduct between parents in the Unit. It involved a surreal comparison between their children's cancers, and is like "Keeping up with the Joneses", where two people boast about their material wealth.

"We've just bought the latest top range Jaguar, isn't it time you replaced your Mercedes?"

"No new car for us this year because we're going cruising round the Seychelles for three months."

A related but disturbing exchange often occurred between two parents from different families in the Unit, as they strived to prove their child has the worst illness and symptoms.

"My daughter has phaeochromocytoma and the added complication of severe hemorrhagic cystitis."

"My son has pancreatoblastoma. It's very, very rare."

Rarity is at a premium here. The rarer the better; more points for rare.

"Yes, but I heard he's doing well. My daughter may never play basketball again."

I thought these peculiar exchanges resulted from living in an affluent district where pettiness is common. However, the catchment for the Royal Marsden covers southern England and includes many poorer neighbourhoods. Is this reaction a subconscious plea for help? Your child's cancer is the worst trauma imaginable, but expressing your desperation to other parents is sometimes futile because they are in the same or a worse position. I found it difficult not to become caught up in these challenges, and this repeated sad little vignette upset me. The competitiveness of the outside world has wormed its way into this beleaguered elite. Why? What good can come from it?

This behaviour does not occur between parents of the relapsed, because they have seen it before and know better. Having lived with these illnesses for too long, they exist on a different plane and grasp the irrefutable score;

Cancer - Two, You - Nil. They have no time for this trivial game playing. You listen to discussions about the complications of a child's disease and realise, despite the smiles and laughter, everyone is in an exceptionally precarious position. These friendly expressions belie considerable pain, grief, and suffering. There is no certainty. Children admitted for their first malignancy die, those admitted for a relapse live. In between these extremes, some live and some die.

Different families often discuss their children's respective diseases, which initially in our case resulted in disbelief and horror after Max's second diagnosis. When later questioned, I decided not to destroy any hope and withheld details of his multiple cancers, and just said that my son had a tumour. However, one father wanted candid details, and I always replied honestly when asked direct questions regarding Max's illnesses. We discussed Methicillin-resistant staphylococcus aureus (MRSA), a bacterial infection resistant to most antibiotics and life-threatening in a cancer ward. His son had just received a brain tumour diagnosis and had contracted MRSA soon after arrival at the Unit. I offered encouragement by recounting Max's successful recovery from this illness. The parent pressed me, and I narrated a potted history of Max's cancers. Afterwards he replied, "I was despondent until I talked to you, but I never thought it could get to this." Nor did I. When the conversation began, I realised he needed someone to talk to and was looking for consolation. Although the resulting chat did not supply the solace he sought, it helped him realise that there were other children in a far worse state than his own.

Nurses and doctors surround these distraught families and hold sway over their child's balancing act between life and death. I found the staff to be exceptional in their jobs, but do not believe they comprehend what happens under these circumstances, despite their proximity to so many cases. They predict reactions but can never fully understand how it feels to be a parent of a child with cancer. That sad honour only applies to those members of the select little community of families within the Unit.

Treatment

Chapter 3

We were introduced to the complexities of cancer a few days after the initial shock of Max's leukaemia. Successful treatment is the Holy Grail and salvation every parent seeks at the end of the rainbow. It gives you hope, but you soon realise unforeseen pitfalls litter the paths to this distant treasure. We became familiar with the procedures, the arcane magic of the doctors, and the jargon of children's cancer. Realising we had lots to learn, we learned quickly, but these were unlike any lessons ever experienced before. This is no simple journey. The consultant described the disease and its therapy, and we thanked him for his explanations. The basics were fine, but our former knowledge counted for little, and we entered a dancing mirror world where events ceased to make any sense. This follows hard on the fact that nothing makes much sense after your child's diagnosis.

After Max's admission to hospital, our consultant discussed the forthcoming treatment with us.

"Allan, I must let you know that some drugs we'll be giving Max for his leukaemia could induce an unrelated cancer."

This statement is incredibly daunting when you solely focus on a cure. How could treatment involve a chemotherapy that might cause a second cancer? Soon you realise that unlike the real world, this is one of uncommon sense.

"Where's the logic there?"

"These drugs may well save Max from his illness, and that's our primary aim. We can't take future cancers into consideration, because if we don't treat him then he'll die. Despite the slight chances of reoccurrence, chemotherapy treatment is the only choice. We must treat his current cancer and treat for survival."

When put in such stark terms, you see his perspective. We had no other option because the Royal Marsden offered the best treatment available; end of story. I believed it then, and I believe it now.

In this reductionist and scientific age, experts give their specialist opinions, and we take them at their word. But this stance is waning, and the public health scares regarding E. Coli and Salmonella have quashed these notions. We expect the medics to know, but why should they? They are not dealing with a car and a faulty alternator or engine with blown gaskets, but with the human body and cancer. They treat illnesses which often have unknown causes, and the progress of these diseases depends on complex genetic switches. The resulting treatments with chemotherapy in 1993 resembled attempts to crack a nut with an atomic pile driver. Doctors confront complications arising at every twist and turn as they coax the body's ability to fight back. This requires the harnessing of a complex immune system and other poorly understood biological processes to keep their patients alive.

The concepts of positive and negative are not absolute in children's cancer treatment. Doing well may mean nothing, and doing badly might be meaningless too, at least in the greater scheme of things. These statements sound confusing and bewilder parents but become more understandable with further explanation. These options are not blurred in normal experience; they are mutually exclusive. Not so in medicine, but this is an issue with our understanding as opposed to the vocation. We want certainty and the doctors to say, "I am God, and have a total comprehension of the body." However, they are human and do their best but cannot work in this world of absolutes. Not yet or for a long time, and they may never meet this stringent stipulation.

The effects of this paradox become obvious when doctors test for defects in intricate body processes. What is the problem? These tests, despite being the best available, are sometimes incorrect because they are not precise enough. On other occasions they cannot cope with the many complicated aspects of illness. A test declaring your child free of a condition may not mean it has disappeared, but just a failure to detect it. While eagerly awaiting test results, familiarisation with treatment makes you realise these are pointers, and you grow wary of taking their outcomes at face value. This caution applies to diagnosis and makes life hard for both doctors and parents alike.

Remission is the term used when the clinicians pronounce you free from illness, and it too has these contradictions. If tests declare your child clear of cancer in the bone marrow, then this only means they cannot detect the disease. Reoccurrence is always possible; it takes a few surviving cells. Remission suggests eradication but is based on a balance of probabilities and not certainty. Treatment ends after consolidation, and many unfamiliar with cancer regard this as synonymous with cure. This conviction is valid for lots of illnesses, but this is not necessarily the case with cancer. It can be difficult explaining this to those outside the Unit. People often accused me of being pessimistic and told me not to consider the likelihood of a relapse. I was not being negative, but just facing reality.

The patient's wellbeing during treatment introduces another curious paradox. With most illnesses, healthiness indicates the effectiveness in resolving a disease. This guideline does not apply with cancer, because outward appearances often only reflect tolerance to the medication and its associated complications. Looking healthy does not necessarily signal success, and the patient's condition can lead to two extremes. Children sometimes appear well during chemotherapy but die because it has been ineffective. Alternatively, they may be exceptionally ill throughout the treatment, but cured because the therapy has worked. It is difficult for everyone concerned to differentiate between these two options.

When the nurses explained this to us, I thought I would be able to stand back dispassionately. Spotting the difference between successful treatment and the effects of the drugs seemed obvious. Sometimes this was true, but usually such detachment was a sham. As a parent, you focus on the current condition of your child, but you must keep reminding yourself that this is superficial. Regular scans or tests for cancer markers signpost the course of the disease, and these are the milestones parents consider relevant.

Treatment is normally the avenging angel that cuts down the disease and restores health. But childhood cancer therapy is a double-edged sword offering hope on one hand and death on the other. It is extremely dangerous and can lead to complications that strike you down as easily as the illness. Some drugs are horrendous, such as the chemotherapy derived from mustard gas, which was used as a chemical weapon in World War One. Doctors deliver this medication using a glass syringe because it dissolves the more common plastic ones. Max received this and other dangerous drugs, which left me ambivalent to treatment.

Max's prescription of diamorphine to ease his pain horrified me. Known as heroin to the world at large, I questioned the use of this dangerous painkiller for my fragile son. The spectre of addiction came to mind, but he had received far more serious medication and this drug could relieve his suffering. My responses were irrational, and a case of my everyday opinions colliding with those of treatment.

Children's cancer therapy differs from other illnesses where you passively bow to the doctors' greater knowledge, because consultants often ask parents to determine their child's future treatment. Strict procedures, known as protocols, control the management of childhood cancer within the specialist units. Hospitals coordinate these nationally and sometimes throughout Europe. The scarcity of these diseases requires this rigorous evaluation, because judging treatment success between limited occurrences of a rare cancer is difficult for a single centre.

Evolving prospective treatments requires combining feedback from existing regimes with the results of clinical and laboratory research. Researchers then propose new therapies as experimental studies for those children most likely to benefit, often those most at risk using the current regimens. Strict protocols control participant selection in these studies to ensure consistency of patients and application of the treatment. Rigorous monitoring also affects the analysis and conclusions regarding the outcome of the trial. The contribution by children undergoing experimental procedures is vital in gauging the viability as an accepted general therapy. If an existing research study applies, then parents may have the choice of submitting their child for a trial. These decisions are amongst the hardest I have ever taken.

Our consultant proposed a bone marrow transplant for Max. In 1993, hospitals only did this after a relapse, but research suggested it might prevent a return of the cancer when used in standard treatment. We opted to take part because we did not want the guilt from denying him the smallest improvement in his chances of survival. Parents need to weigh the potential gains versus the risks, but these questions have no answer because they are those being studied.

In a controlled study some children receive the trial treatment, and the rest stay on the existing therapy to enable a comparison between the two. A computer randomises the possibilities, so no one involved in the investigation can introduce any form of bias. In our case Max remained on his current regimen, leaving Sara and I extremely relieved he did not undergo transplant because we dreaded the prospect of this dangerous procedure. We had absolved ourselves by putting him forward for a trial, because we had gotten our preferred choice despite giving him the chance of having experimental treatment. If he were to die, then we could not blame ourselves for never taking the offer of the new therapy.

Our morbid fear of transplants soon faded during Max's second cancer, and in treatment you often find yourself on ground you never expected to reach. These are places where the unthinkable becomes transformed into the desirable. What first appear as straws in the sea later become rafts of hope. Your perspective changes as the disease develops, and any option becomes a glowing light at the end of the tunnel when presented with the prospect of your child's death.

Max's transplant consisted of a bone marrow infusion followed by extremely high dose chemotherapy, which carried the risk of organ damage. When I asked the consultants how they assessed the required dosage, they replied that they did not yet have precise guidelines. Despite having an estimate of the measure tolerated by most children, they did not have enough information to gauge fatal doses in individual cases. We were between a rock and a hard place; potential death if you opt for the treatment, potential death if you do not. The consultant said they would give higher concentrations of the drugs, but we did not realise to what extent. The first drug was twelve times stronger than the standard dose and started crystallising in Max's Hickman Lines. Two of the three lines developed blockages and clogging of the third would require an operation. Fortunately, several minutes later the nurse cleared the line, and he did not need surgery.

Complications are dimensions of treatment that may be as lethal as the disease itself. Minor infections can be fatal to the immunosuppressed, and parents are vigilant about the health of visitors. Chicken pox is particularly dangerous, because the symptoms are not obvious until well after contracting the illness. If an infected child visited the Unit in the incubation period, then a general consternation spread amongst the families. This led to intense cross examination of all children and siblings alike, to discover whether anyone else had become ill.

Paula contracted chicken pox midway through Max's second treatment and vomited over the back seat as I drove to the Marsden. I could not help her while driving, despite her extreme upset and obvious sickness. On arriving at the hospital, Sara and I cleaned the car before she returned home with Paula.

The doctors forbade Paula's subsequent entry into the Unit, which created logistical problems while we took turns nursing Max. For the following ten days Paula visited but remained outside, and it was difficult for our concerned four-year-old to understand why she could not see her brother. We wheeled him to reception in his wheelchair, and they waved to each other and blew kisses through the glass window separating them.

As mentioned previously, Max contracted MRSA within two weeks of his first admission. This bacterium, which is resistant to most antibiotics and known as "Golden Staph", is the bane of hospitals and can be lethal to both normal and immunosuppressed patients. Another thunderbolt. Did we have a copper rod reaching high into the heavens designed to attract these massive discharges of ill fortune? No, like many families, we were just unlucky during Max's treatment. Out of the clear blue sky came complications we had never even conceived. Golden Staph was rare when he had his leukaemia but has since spread throughout hospitals worldwide.

Six months after his second diagnosis and when at home, Max complained of an itching foot. While examining him, a slight reddening raised my concern. Twenty minutes later he moaned in pain, and on seeing further inflammation we went to the hospital straightaway. A doctor administered antibiotics late that evening and we returned home. My uneasiness grew when I spotted red tendrils creeping along the veins in his foot, so I decided to sleep on the floor of his room to monitor the infection. He slept restlessly, so I took his temperature and discovered he had a fever. I drove Max back to the Unit at two o'clock in the morning, and he received a blood platelet transfusion and stronger antibiotics. I drank coffee and watched him through the night while sitting next to his hospital bed. He started hallucinating.

"Daddy, who's written this book?"

"What book, Maxie, what do you mean?"

"The ward looks like a big open book, and who are those strange people? Perhaps I'm imagining things, but it's very scary."

I calmed him and administered paracetamol, which reduced his temperature. The following morning, he said he had seen dying bodies falling to the floor from the pages of an enormous book. As they hit the ground their ghosts rose to the ceiling. The progress of the infection frightened me because the two fine lines had traversed across his foot and began moving up his leg. Wary, I still had confidence the doctors could bring it under control, though it took a week of first line antibiotics before he responded to the medication. In hindsight, this and similar complications seemed unreal, but were similar to the other hurdles we had faced. Only on reflection does one realise the extremes confronted while nursing a child with cancer.

Max had several complications throughout his illnesses, but we were no different to most other families within the Unit. Complications are various and include amputation, blindness, drug intolerance, transfusion reactions, and organ breakdown. The full list is lengthy and may or may not affect a child. Often these problems extend long after treatment has ended, because chemotherapy is a vicious medication and often causes severe damage to a growing body. The costs can be enormous. One boy, the most mischievous I ever knew, developed breathing difficulties and contracted meningitis after a transplant. I met the same boy two years later, and he had become a shadow of the youth I had known. He had learning disabilities, and the treatment had impaired his growth and eroded his vital self-confidence. Likewise, major transplant complications affected many other children.

Parents crave something to cling to throughout their child's cancer; numbers or a framework for their fragmented existence. You want facts you can mull over and tell people to make it real and tangible. These are the percentages, and parents instinctively ask, "What are the chances of my child's survival?" This is possibly the hardest question for a consultant to answer, and yet another feature in this sorry saga. Percentages are fingers in the wind, guesses reflecting a rough average based on previous cases of the cancer. They are useful to cradle and mentally caress, especially when every day brings unexpected leaps forward or backward in your child's illness. They serve their purpose well until there are no percentages left. Whether they are correct is irrelevant; they give parents a fix on the grey and shifting world of their child's cancer.

Outsiders took the perspective that all was well after Max completed his leukaemia treatment. Not so. For two and a half years we lived with a 50% possibility of his survival, not a useful percentage when contemplating your child's future. I used to stare into the night sky, trying to make sense of this figure and its consequences on my son's life. A surreal scenario often came to mind, in which I imagined a discussion with the Great Accountant. If given a theoretical choice, would I want to know the ultimate outcome and avoid the torture of waiting to see if Max would die?

"Well, my son, I believe you have a special request."

"Yes, Your Holiness, can you tell me whether Max will survive?"

"Time will tell, my son, time will tell."

"I haven't been a bad person, couldn't you just let me know now? What's the difference? Ultimately, it'll turn out the same, but at least we can prepare ourselves. Please give this consideration, because I've never asked anything from you before?"

"Hmm, how irregular, but I see your point. Okay, I'll make this an exception on the condition you don't tell anybody else. I can't have this as a precedent, because who knows where it would lead? Chaos, no doubt. I might get parents querying their child's future health even before conception, which would be a bureaucratic nightmare. Go ahead, toss this coin."

A golden coin fell from the sky.

"You want me involved in the decision?"

"Of course, you have to do some of the work."

I catch the coin, flip it, and it spins for two eternities.

"Heads."

It lands tails up. Living with a 50% chance of survival over the long-term is difficult, but no one suggested otherwise.

We went for Max's third check-up and received confirmation the tests could not detect any leukaemia cells. Elated, I dropped my guard, and the psychological wall erected to protect me against his death crumbled. It looked as if we might cheat these odds and Max would survive. The maelstrom had sucked us into the vortex many times, but now we could relax and stop worrying. He received his second cancer diagnosis two months later.

Survival percentages are like infinity; theoretical and difficult to grasp. I introduced Max to this concept when he was six years old. It amazed him and took a short while before he understood the idea.

"Dad, what's the biggest number?"

"There isn't one, the numbers just keep increasing."

"But there must be."

"No, Maxie, if you add one to a number, then you get another."

"Well, when does that reach the largest?"

"It doesn't, it continues on and on forever."

We tried it out. He gave me a number, and I added one, and he soon understood.

"That's amazing. I mean you think they'd stop, but they just keep on getting bigger."

Max's second cancer had two subtypes of tumour, and the survival rates at the time were 60% and 30% respectively. Percentages once more came to the fore. After we received the news that the disease had spread to his spine, I passed our first leukaemia consultant in the corridor. He stopped to say how sorry he was at this latest setback.

"What are the percentages for Max's survival now? 20%? 10%?"

"Allan, I don't think discussing percentages is helpful. When it comes down to it, they're meaningless, because the only thing relevant is whether Max survives. Some children make amazing recoveries; others fall by the wayside when we've given them a good chance. Try to think positively and ignore the numbers."

Still I persisted, and only with hindsight did I realise the futility of my questions.

"Okay, I understand, but if you were to give a number what would it be?"

He did not reply, so I pressed him further. "5%?"

"Yes, possibly somewhere in that region."

Sara and I pushed this minimal possibility of survival to the back of our minds. Coming to terms with such thin chances is inconceivable, and so we lived our lives from day to day and the numbers drifted into the background. A frightful dividing line exists between black and white options in childhood cancer; your child either survives or dies. The period spent living between these two extremes is an unimaginable torment for lots of parents while they wait and hope. For years and years. Possibly only a bereaved parent can draw this distinction, because many mothers and fathers cannot afford to contemplate the unthinkable, and their only thought is "My child will survive."

After Max's tumour diagnosis, I wanted to know if his first and second cancers were in any way associated. This knowledge would have made no material difference, but I needed to grasp this information. The annual chances of a child of his age having Acute Myeloid Leukaemia were ten in a million, and around four in a million for Rhabdomyosarcoma. The likelihood of independently contracting both illnesses within a four-year period were incomprehensible, and so I assumed a correlation existed between the two cancers. I started doing the lottery every week, because although the possibility of winning is about one in seventy million, we had encountered probabilities close to this order of magnitude.

Max's cancer treatments involved three consultancies, which is unusual but occurred because separate consultants supervised the leukaemias and tumours. The third was the Professor in charge of the Unit, and he oversaw both of Max's treatments. A parent's relationship with their specialist requires mutual faith and understanding. We had that rapport, and they and the nurses became trusted friends. The consultant needs to judge how much parents understand and at what level to pitch any discussion with them. Do they have the emotional capacity to absorb the imparted information? From Sara's and my perspective, we wanted clarity and explanations for any specific symptom or scenario. Irrespective of the consequences, Sara and I considered this honesty paramount because it would help us grasp our degree of uncertainty. We asked searing questions and received candid answers. This is not always the norm, because consideration of each case is necessary based on its circumstances. Not every family wants or can cope with the detail.

Discussions between consultants and parents sometimes lead to misinterpretation. I used to take a notebook and log what I thought I had heard. Simple, but not true. Several times Sara and I attended consultations but left with diametrically opposite impressions of what the consultant had said. You often hear what you want to hear, and despite agreeing on a statement's content, we interpreted it differently. For this reason, a nurse is always present so you can ask questions afterwards.

Soon after the official diagnosis for Max's tumour, we had a meeting with our leukaemia consultant. He did not mention the new cancer, which surprised me given his caring manner during the endless waiting. Later I asked him why and he apologised, saying the news had distressed him and he just could not face talking about Max's second disease during the consultation. This admission showed the personal impact on him, despite the suffering he saw every day.

Another event, this time involving a nurse, stands out vividly and occurred while nursing Max during a potent dose of medication. The drug resulted in extreme sickness and pain. He vomited about four or five times a day and urinated many times during the night. Despite his pain, he refused offers of oral morphine because of the taste and declined the intravenous line due to its discomfort. Throughout Max's second cancer, I found it difficult coping with his physical pain. His hurt became mine, and I had no way of blocking my child's suffering. His crying left me heartbroken, helpless, and insignificant. Alice, Max's nurse that day, came to tend him when the throbbing started. As she approached, I glimpsed what I called the "Look." It is the expression where the nurses' professional mask drops momentarily and shows they too have a horror and deep sadness at what they see. I suspect they are not aware of this fleeting lapse. They are the kindest and most compassionate people I have ever met, but they appear to have a regardless superhuman ability to keep caring. Sometimes this used to get to me, but seeing the mask drop revealed her actual feelings. I felt guilty at seeing her emotions, but they were comforting, nonetheless.

These little scenarios were important to me and showed the true mindset of the staff. Perversely, they made me realise we were not alone, and they too are human. I often reflected on the consultants, doctors, nurses, and ourselves; who cares for the carers? Frontline primary cancer workers sometimes suffer burn out, because there is a limit to the emotional onslaught anyone can endure before it affects them. Their patience, care, and immense strength amazed me.

One nurse, Kara, gave Max special attention during his leukaemia. She provided total unconditional love to us, together with other families under her care. It surprised me someone could give so freely and ask nothing in return. I asked her how she kept going, and she replied that if she gave the children 110%, then they returned her love countless times. This payback kept her working for so long and made the role fulfilling. But during Max's second illness, she retired after twenty years in childhood cancer nursing. Her close personal involvement with patients had started to affect her, and she could no longer dissociate herself from the heartache.

During her last day at the hospital, Kara visited Max's bedside and gave him an enormous hug. He had withdrawn into himself because of the pain and would not let anyone near him, but their close relationship enabled her to reach into his depression. As she gently enquired about his aching and anger, Max responded by explaining his misery, and this was the first time he had spoken openly during his second illness. Kara sat and talked with him, validating his emotions, and her ability to elicit responses from him showed her empathy with the children. At Kara's request, they exchanged addresses and telephone numbers, and she said he could ring or send her a letter whenever he wanted. She again selflessly offered her care to a child, despite her own needs to escape childhood cancer and knowing his prognosis and likely outcome.

We considered ourselves honoured to be one of two pairs of parents attending Kara's leaving presentation. Long-term frontline nurses deserve and receive enormous respect, and the praise pouring forth throughout the speeches filled the room with emotion. I found it hard saying my last goodbyes to her and several were close to tears.

The staff have my deepest admiration. Consultants must inform numerous families that nothing more can be done for their child. Irrespective of how case hardened you become; this emotional barrage takes its toll. The doctors and nurses show an incredible dedication and care and do this with little respite. They leave me feeling very humble.

Reactions

Chapter 4

We had been set adrift in the ocean on the Tropic of Cancer. The illness does not solely affect your family, because this sea has waves that ripple far and wide to engulf many others. Friends, relations, and workplace colleagues are unexpectedly brought into close contact with childhood cancer. It becomes real, and often people grasped their fragility and insignificance in the wider scheme of life. Our own and other's responses to Max's disease were mostly those expected, but not always.

Parents have differing coping mechanisms, and during Max's leukaemia Sara and I fell into two disparate camps. I coped from a practical perspective but did not consider her feelings for Max and Paula. At the other extreme, Sara reacted emotionally and lacked practicality for the organisation required when your family fragments without warning. Both reactions are necessary, but in moderation and not in the excessive way we initially responded to the illness. During his next cancer we were more prepared, had learned from our earlier experience, and acquitted ourselves by being more empathetic to each other.

Max's tumour left Sara and I feeling as if we were spectators in someone else's nightmare. The world became unreal, remote, and distanced, and we could not believe this was happening to us. I worried about this defence mechanism that resulted in our dissociation from traumatic events. What would happen when we truly took on board the enormity of our plight? The true significance only sank in two years later. Your perspective becomes distorted while in the eye of the storm, and only when looking back do you understand the full extent of the damage.

After the second diagnosis, Sara and I met the Children's Unit psychologist, added to the staff to help families deal with the onset of their child's disease. While discussing our response to the new cancer, we explained our earlier mistakes and how we intended coping with Max's next treatment. After the original shock we had switched into crisis mode again and packed our bags ready for hospital visits. We discussed our preparations, how we would work alternate shifts, deflect the phone calls, and manage Paula's welfare. The psychologist was surprised by our pre-planning.

"You appear to be approaching Max's cancer as if it's a battle?"

"It is, we've been here before and we've learned. We know to expect the unexpected."

I had many adverse reactions to Max's illness, despite my coping. After his first diagnosis, I split people into two categories; one included us and the desperate little band of families in the Unit, the other consisted of the real world. Coming to terms with this perspective became hard and continued until long after his death.

When walking around town looking at everyone leading their normal lives, I felt I did not belong and as if I was an alien. What did people think when they saw me, given my presence in the milling crowd and apparently no different from the rest? Inside, I had this desperate urge to scream at the top of my voice, "My child has cancer!" I frantically needed to explain how my life had fallen off the edge of an unimaginable cliff. Desperate, I wanted to grab them, shake them, and ask if they knew how it felt to be the parent of a cancer-stricken child.

The constant leukaemia treatment had us at its mercy, and one of my responses was a need for unnatural control. Resenting visitors, I found them an intrusion on my ability to cope, and the phone calls we received also distressed me. Later, Sara and I took turns nursing Max and alternated by spending a night at home, but incessant ringing interrupted those evenings.

People rang for updates and I was grateful for their concern, but they did not realise the strain created by their calls. We often spent hours describing Max's treatment during the previous days to caller after caller. It is demoralising explaining a recent downturn in your child's condition after a sleepless night in the hospital has left you tired and exhausted. After a while we deflected many calls by asking callers to ring our families for the latest news. The phone calls affected me far more than Sara, who found talking to people helped vent her feelings, showing that what helps one person may be unsuitable for another. Eventually I bought an answerphone and would often just let it ring while I tried winding down from the day.

Max's initial admission to the hospital also stressed our two-year-old daughter, Paula. During her first visit to the Unit, she wanted to tuck a teddy into his bed and give him a birthday kiss and present. He was unconscious, having returned from an operation, and she did not understand why he would not wake. Realising no one had explained why, I told her he was asleep because of the medicines, and these would help him get better. After she asked about the Hickman line protruding from his body, I described how the nurses used it to dispense medication. She seemed far happier knowing reasons for her brother's condition, but who can tell what children absorb at that age?

After Max awoke, we told him about Paula's concern, and the next time she visited he said how much he loved her and gave her a big kiss. She responded by giving him her koala teddy; her most treasured possession. Later, she became agitated when he refused his medication, and I suspect she understood my explanation that he needed it to get well again.

Paula was an outgoing child, and her loud infectious laughter and giggles attracted attention wherever she went. Sometimes her vitality was overwhelming when we were frazzled, but often her exuberance galvanised us when Max's condition had deteriorated.

Paula coped well in the face of our family turmoil but sometimes suffered from recurrent nightmares, one involving an earthquake that threatened to engulf us. She had other anxieties, such as fire consuming our house or Sara ageing, presumably with the assumption her mother's life may be under threat.

How does a four-year-old cope with her sibling's second cancer? It was clear Paula understood the gravity of her brother's sudden readmission to hospital. During Max's leukaemia she spent some time living with neighbours, but during his tumour treatment we often returned home, and this helped us stay together as a family. She worshipped her elder sibling, and his absence on her first day at school was upsetting. "I want Max back from the hospital and for us to play together, like other children with brothers," she wailed through a flood of tears.

Many parents have a natural tendency to concentrate on the child with cancer at the expense of their other children. But they should avoid this pitfall because it causes damage to the sibling's development and relationship with the parent. I was guilty of devoting my concentration to Max's wellbeing, and this eventually resulted in a gulf between myself and Paula. She resented my presence and withdrew her affection. Those open wounds only started to heal two years after he died.

On what would have been Max's eleventh birthday, Paula and I went to Cornwall to view the solar eclipse. While travelling we spotted the remnants of an airplane contrail, and the thin bank of cloud curved gracefully to the edge of the horizon. Anna commented, "Dad, look at that path from heaven, perhaps Max will come back and see us?" Slowly she too adjusted to the loss of her brother.

The reactions to childhood cancer by the extended families are as one would expect, and they have a tough time coping. Our relatives were 250 miles away, which aggravated these problems. We described Max's condition when they phoned, because it was foremost in our minds, but did not ring everyone on the resolution of a crisis. Telling everyone concerned about the various nuances was not practical, because we could only just cope with the complications as they arose. Sara and I provided our relations with much more detail compared to anyone else who contacted us. With many people, even close friends, we abbreviated or omitted the details of a specific circumstance because it was too complex to explain. Our families, however, had difficulty understanding the intricacies of any given scenario.

We lived and breathed the complexities of therapy; they did not, and remoteness did not help with their comprehension of the daily changes in Max's health. We were contributing towards his treatment, but our inaccessibility also created issues for them. Our parents felt helpless and had the added disadvantage of remotely watching our suffering.

Friends and relations often visited us, but this sometimes created logistical problems. Time and again, we had to pick them up, take them to the hospital, and feed them. Juggling both the needs of your child with those of others compounds the physical and emotionally exhausting pressure of nursing.

Max's illness left several of our friends afraid for their offspring, and although childhood cancer is rare, it may not appear so when you know an afflicted family. His close pals also suffered badly, because his disease had stripped them of their youthful innocence. Children should not have to face the stark reality of death, especially not of their own kind. Dying happens to "old" people and is not part of a child's existence of dens in the garden, doll's houses, and bike riding. Children's fears include those of the imagination, such as ogres, sandmen, and dinosaurs. Those terrors live in the dark places, in nightmares and hidden corners under the stairs, but such fears should never show their face in the real world.

Most outside the family responded with care and sympathy to Max's cancer, but this was not always the case. Breaking the news of a child's illness to people who have no inkling of what has happened is common for parents. The resulting vignettes are like scenes from a sick farce. The person receiving the details cannot cope and often ends up in tears. You then find yourself both consoling and helping them come to terms with your problem. The first time this occurred was unsettling, but we soon became used to this reaction.

Another common response experienced widely by parents is denial by friends, acquaintances, and strangers. People today experience tragedies second or third hand, and frequently only encounter suffering through various forms of media. The potential death of a child has ceased being part of our worldview in the last couple of generations. But this is not the case in countries where families still lose at least one or more children. We have lost touch in the West and often discount daily news reports because they occur elsewhere and are not our problem. The reality rarely affects you, but when it does, it can be too much to bear. Denial is a reaction to events we cannot understand, and some people avoided me throughout and after Max's leukaemia. I suspect they did not know what to say because it lay outside their framework. It was outside ours too. We had no training, nor went on that imaginary course "Childhood Cancer: How to cope if it strikes."

The denial sometimes manifested itself by a total disregard when Max's cancer arose in conversation, as if we had announced our son had a nasty cough. I can only assume the other person worried that any mention of his disease might upset us, or that its reality was too horrific to accept. The former instance is ludicrous when examined in the cold light of day. We had lived with our son's cancer for many years and mentioning his illness could not offend us; our lives revolved around this sole focus. Saying something, anything, is preferential to staying silent. The words may not be right, sound awkward or be inadequate, but confronting a cancer or bereavement is better than pretending it does not exist. The alternative of denial can be selfish and hurtful.

Sara and I experienced diverse reactions and disturbing behaviours from people who showed a complete absence of empathy. One occurred with a friend visiting us after our return home from the hospital during Max's tumour treatment. We explained the gravity of Max's illness to him, but our words fell on deaf ears. It was difficult to tell whether he was being insensitive or had just not listened to us. He remarked on how stressed I looked and suggested we move out into the countryside, which he assumed would be helpful for Max's cancer. At one point he commented, "Well, the outlook seems hopeful for this illness." We looked drained because every three or four days in the previous weeks had resulted in a lurch further into the morass, and we were not making any headway. Our son had a second and different cancer with a minimal hope of cure, and we were confronting the unthinkable.

Two more occasions of complete lack of human understanding involved religion, and both were inexcusable. I am not religious but respect those who keep their beliefs personal. Many people use their faith to get through each day and as a basis behind leading an upright and moral existence. I understand this perspective, and some have earned my highest esteem based on how they interpret their religion and live their lives. There is also the religion of zealots, fools, and bigots, whose followers feel compelled to show others the error of their ways. This lack of toleration rejects the fuzzy imprecision of real life.

A member of Sara's extended family sent us a letter that said she was thinking of us and that her fellow churchgoers were praying for Max. Several other letters had expressed a similar message, and we were profoundly grateful these unknown communities had found a place in their hearts for us. This letter, however, declared that prayers had delivered him from his leukaemia, and that their congregation would also save him from his second cancer. It continued by suggesting Max was only alive because of their love of God and that the doctors' efforts were meaningless. The letter included a "miracle card" showing a picture of Jesus, and she told us that Max would recover if we kept it near his bed. I threw up my hands in desperation with this complete lack of empathy. I knew the love and care we had given to our son, and the patience and dedication displayed by the hospital staff. Max had crawled through crisis after crisis before emerging from his treatment. The insensitivity of this correspondence gave me an opportunity to vent my anger, and I furiously ripped up the card. I initially intended destroying the letter but thought this might upset Sara.

The second offensive religious letter was almost laughable and had been sent by a childhood friend of mine. His life as a teenager had fallen apart because of drugs and alcohol, but he found salvation by becoming a born-again Christian. Sara and I read it with incredulity and consigned it to the bin. The four-page letter started like many others sent to us. He and his wife were horrified to hear about Max's tumour, but the letter rankled when they said they knew how we felt. One consistent message from everybody else was they could not imagine our feelings. From this point the letter went downhill at an accelerating pace. It said my dissolute lifestyle during my adolescence had caused Max's illness, and only my turning towards God would lead to our redemption. Three pages detailed why and how I could repent, but my failure to respond would have consequences. I wondered after Max died whether they genuinely believed that my rejection of God justified Max's death. I drew two conclusions from this missive. It is sad that people, whatever their religious persuasion, find it necessary to impose their views on others. Secondly, it is unforgivable this correspondence preyed on a family at its lowest moment in its existence and used hope as a lure for conversion. These letters were abhorrent and insulting.

Another incident showing crass and inconsiderate behaviour surprisingly involved a member of the medical profession. I visited a specialist because I sometimes could not merge images from both eyes. Unlike most people, my brain performed this function, and I lapsed into double vision when tired or stressed. The doctor said I could have an operation but recommended I live with the condition because of the associated risks. He told me other sufferers often lived a lifestyle involving an unhealthy diet and too much stress at work, which were all part of the destructive regime of our modern society. He questioned me likewise, and I supplied relevant replies. To explain my symptoms, I told him that my problems had only appeared during my son's leukaemia treatment. The ophthalmologist did not blink an eyelid and continued talking for five minutes with a messianic fervour about how I should change my way of life. His total lack of empathy and the utter indifference of his tirade left me stunned and too numb to argue. I mentioned this incident to a sympathetic nurse after the consultation, who said that he always gave this lecture to his patients.

Despite these inconsiderate events, most showed exceptional empathy because imagining themselves in our position filled them with horror. The compassion shown throughout Max's illness uplifted us, especially when people we did not know took the trouble to send caring and heart-warming correspondence full of consideration. We received long and touching letters from friends of friends moved by our plight. Many also repeatedly sent flowers, looked after Paula, cooked meals, or did our washing and ironing. These were practical and helpful self-sacrificing acts that raised my faith in humanity. This kindness led to an odd paradox. The psychological walls were there for the tough times, and we fought back and tried to carry on with our lives. This is a natural reaction, but these acts of kindness, unsolicited care, and unselfish gestures left us defenceless. On occasions we found ourselves unable to hold this consideration at arm's length, and people's thoughtfulness brought us close to tears. Their efforts were humbling, and we felt almost guilty at accepting help. We were deeply grateful and still are; they made an enormous difference.

We saw the best and worst of human nature during Max's illnesses. Both were surprising in their extremes.

Medication

Chapter 5

My role as a father changed once Max became embroiled in his leukaemia treatment, but never in my wildest nightmares would I have envisaged myself as a Torturer. I am not cruel on any level, but this fate often befalls the parent dispensing the pills and changing the dressings. It results in cajoling or even quarrelling with the child to achieve these tasks. In this strange paradoxical world of childhood cancer, you battle with the person you love the most, because you love them so much. Sometimes it must be you because despite the conflicts, you are the only one trusted by your child. Parents want to do as much as practical but are caught between the devil and the deep blue sea. Your child suffers if he does not take the medication, and you suffer during the battles.

Why do parents take on this task? It occurs because of the considerable work involved in looking after a child with cancer, and hospitals struggle to cope without this help. The basic roles, such as comforting or giving a sick child medicine, can be very time consuming. Parental contribution is crucial in these circumstances and frees up the nurses to do the rest of their vital functions.

We administered Max's oral medicines, and it was exhausting overseeing thirty-one medications a day at home during his second cancer. I needed him to take this mix of tablets and liquids at specific times, but a refused dose or missed deadline became problematic. These delays were stressful because I worried about the potential effects caused by the lack of treatment, together with the shortage of time before the next dose. Prolonged hold ups meant waking Max at night, which left him indignant and angry. Cancer had invaded his life and interrupting an already disturbed sleep was often the last straw. Childhood cancer victims have had their normal carefree lives replaced with confusion and pain. It is common for them to refuse drugs, dressing changes, or any other form of treatment as a reaction to these intrusions.

On one occasion while at home, I helped our community nurse spend hours trying to remove a dressing from our sick and angry son. Max did not want anyone near the tender area after his operation, and eventually we removed the adhesive dressing by force.

"Dad, I never ever want you near me again."

I had become the Torturer's Accomplice and betrayed him by helping in the one thing he dreaded. His fear was justified, because detaching the very sticky plaster was painful, but failure to do so might have led to a life-threatening infection.

What state have you reached when you start cutting deals with your young son? These were the complicated treatment agreements between Max and me that were required to keep him healthy. They involved my coaxing to get him to take the next set of medication, and his consequent bargaining to create delays by imposing unreasonable terms. The pacts were time limited and needed agreement and action before the onset of the ensuing deadline.

Max wanted leverage against these impositions to gain a modicum of control, which resulted in the refusal of painkillers and the downside of his consequent suffering. This led to a repeated difficult standoff, and I said I would not sit and listen to his cries if he did not take the tablets. I hated it, because I knew the pills could alleviate his pain. Sometimes I walked away from the confrontation and waited until he asked for the medication, and only after the aching subsided did we become friends again. At what cost do you act out this role of Torturer? At the time I endured resolutely, but in the longer term these clashes incurred heavy emotional costs on me.

Eventually, as far as the painkillers were concerned, I ignored the guidelines and instead let him decide when to take the morphine. I told him how much the battling upset me and given that he was the one in pain, then he could choose if or when to relieve it. I said he needed to have the doses regularly, and that they did not work instantaneously or have any effect without a consistency of dose. Although this may sound radical to an observer, it helped. On regaining control, Max requested the pills, and we started working together again. I used this ploy in the future and the removal of coercion made him far more receptive to medication.

This laissez-faire strategy did not work with crucial medicines having no obvious effect. For example, potassium tablets do not ease any symptoms but prevent potential heart attacks caused by the side effects of chemotherapy. Max used to bargain with me for hours to avoid taking his potassium pills. On one occasion he agreed to have them after a bath, but I knew full well this was just another delaying tactic. It was time to confront the issue.

"Max, we've got to sort this out. We need to discuss why you must take your medicines."

"Because the doctors tell you to give them to me," he muttered sullenly.

"Yes, but they prescribe the drugs to help you recover from the illness."

"I don't feel ill at the moment."

"The potassium doesn't stop you feeling unwell, but if you don't have it, then you might die."

This was long before he realised his illness could be fatal.

"Whoa!" he exclaimed in that funny way of his that signalled extreme surprise.

"Really real?" This was what Max said when I told him something outrageous, which he suspected to be complete garbage, but was part of the teasing and banter between us.

"Yes, really real. If you stop taking the potassium, then you might have a heart attack. Your arguing about the medicines is good, because it shows you've still got the strength to fight, but we need to work together to get you through your cancer. You should fight the illness and not me. These rows upset us and lead nowhere because you eventually take the tablets, which makes the quarrelling pointless. I hate having these fights with you and only do it because I love you and want to stop the pain and hurt. These arguments are unpleasant, and I realise you dislike the pills. They taste horrible and are difficult to swallow, but I want to help you beat the cancer."

"Okay Dad. I'm sorry and I'll try to take them in future."

The fights did not end, but this was the start of the growing trust and bond that helped us both through treatment. Having first checked with the nurses, I tried a few of the more innocuous medicines. Liquid potassium tastes foul, and the laxative called Lactulose is disgustingly sweet, and I understood his aversion to these medications.

Early in the medicine battles, Sara and I used to conceal ground pills in Max's food to disguise their taste, but with many it broke through the mask. After a while we realised these underhand tactics were not a good idea. Deception can cause children to lose faith and hope in their sole perceived lifeline; their parents. Above everything else, they need love, trust, and care. You must supply all these and more.

Chemotherapy kills rapidly reproducing cells and is often successful in treating cancer, but it has the unfortunate side effect of eradicating other normal ones that duplicate quickly. This primarily affects those lining the mouth and intestinal tract. Their damage can lead to opportunistic infection when naturally occurring bacteria attack their compromised host. The children must take special solutions, known as the "swills, to disinfect their mouths and gut to counter the effects of bacterial and fungal infections. Patients rub their teeth and gums with soft sponge swabs, because toothbrushes cause harm to the tender lining of the mouth. Max struggled with this cleansing and hated using the sponges. I tried them; they were unpleasant and caused me to retch.

"Max, you must rinse with the swills."

"Why, it tastes horrible and at least I'm doing the brushing now? Surely that's much better than before?"

"Do you understand why you need the swills?"

"Yes, I'll get a sore mouth if I don't use them."

"That's right, and it's why Pedro is so ill."

The child in question had also refused the mouthwash and had severe oral infections. A large abscess on his lip and white pustulous sores lining the inside of his mouth resulted in eating difficulties and consequent other complications. Max had seen Pedro's ulcers and took note. "Okay, I'll take the swills."

I talked with another family having similar problems persuading their daughter to take medicine. I queried whether they thought encouragement from a peer might be better than from a parent, nurse, or doctor. They were prepared to try anything, and so I approached Max and asked for his help. Honoured by the request, he talked to the girl in the presence of her parents and me, but to no avail. I suggested the adults retire into the background and requested Max's help again. He spent ten minutes trying to convince her, but his endeavours were unsuccessful. Disappointed, we returned to his bedroom, but later that day she resumed her medication.

These children grow up years before their time and it took us a while to realise Max needed total honesty. Parents have an innate need to shield their child from the stark truths of cancer treatment, but children need to understand why these procedures exist and how they affect their lives. Sara and I encountered events we could never have imagined prior to the illness. Parents and children start treatment with reference to the outside world, and this is only natural because they have no other. You slowly realise your child is no longer the one you knew before the disease, and that you too have also changed. Both sides adjust and this alteration of frames of reference is necessary for everyone's sake. We learned that honesty always helped. I suspect this may not suit every family, but it forged a deep trust between ourselves and Max, and I am thankful we took this path.

Freedom

Chapter 6

We had the chance to take Max home for a break after ten weeks of leukaemia treatment. Sara and I packed his toys and prepared ourselves by collecting our belongings, but we were too cynical to celebrate this opportunity to return. There had been many earlier occasions where the doctors told us we could leave the Unit but rescinded the decision a few hours later. Max was extremely susceptible to infections, and often his temperature suddenly rocketed, or a test detected bacteria just as we were due to leave. We had little notice on this occasion because the medical staff did not want to elevate our expectations. Despite their reservations, we had our hopes raised and dashed, and had to stay for two more days. Jubilant when we eventually left the hospital, we sang in the car all the way home.

Nearly four hours after our return, I saw Max briefly shudder. I felt uneasy because I had never witnessed a momentary tremor, though had seen the rigor shivering which precedes a high fever. Despite him looking healthy, I took his temperature. Nothing was amiss. Most parents have an instinctive child-radar, but it becomes super-tuned when your child has cancer. Intuitive and correct most of the time, my gut instinct did not trust what I had glimpsed.

We returned to the Unit, and Max started running around manically as he played with the other children. The confused doctor asked why we had returned, and I sheepishly expressed my concerns. On occasions such as this you question your grip on reality. On the one hand you act as expected for a parent, on the other you need to gauge the symptoms you see from a dispassionate and medical perspective. A fine line exists between sheer false panic and having a genuine reason for alarm. It is not easy.

The nurse could not find any overt problem, but as a precaution decided to cleanse Max's Hickman Line before taking a blood sample. As she flushed the tube, he shook and became subdued. Rapidly deteriorating, within minutes he began shutting down both mentally and physically. The nurses instantly recognised the crisis; a line infection. The flushing had pumped pathogens throughout his body, which resulted in instant blood poisoning. This is very frightening, and Max had experienced it once beforehand. A nurse injected intensive first line antibiotics and sat at his bedside taking his pulse and declaring his heart rate every minute, as other staff came to help. No machines in this scenario; because it requires intelligent assessment, time is crucial, and each second counts. As the minutes ticked by, he sank towards coma.

Much later, after Max's condition had stabilised, the examining nurse asked me how I had detected the infection. I replied that I had purely acted instinctively, but there were other occasions where I behaved likewise but misinterpreted his symptoms.

During Max's treatment for his second cancer, he awoke in the middle of the night oblivious to his surroundings.

"Daddy, why have we changed wards? I don't remember moving beds."

"We haven't changed beds Maxie, it's the same bed you were in when you went to sleep."

He became distressed and scared.

"What's happening to the walls, why are they moving? Who are those people watching me? Why are we in a cave Daddy? Please take me back to the Marsden."

"No, Maxie, we're still in the hospital. Look, here's the curtain round your bed."

Max had cancer in his spine, and my major worry was the disease reaching his brain. I had visions of his impending death and did not want to see my child dying as a vegetable. Sitting there probing your son's hallucination is frightening, because you wonder whether it signifies the next thunderbolt. Many thoughts race through your mind as you try to understand the symptoms and their implications. I rushed out of the ward, breathless and panicking, and ran headlong into the young standby registrar. Despite my demented anxiety, he calmly examined Max and said a fever had caused the symptoms. This helped not one jot. I had made correct assessments several times in the past, so drank coffee throughout the night and watched Max like a hawk. He was fine the following day, but the lack of sleep left me in tatters.

We were nervous of the path ahead after leaving the Unit on conclusion of over three and a half months of continuous leukaemia treatment. I rang the doctor a week later and during the conversation explained that the hospital had recently released us. She jokingly reprimanded me.

"The Royal Marsden doesn't release patients, we discharge them. Release is a term used for prisoners."

"We were there for nearly four months, it felt like a release."

Some of the biggest problems faced by families occur at the end of treatment, because the return to normal life is like a severing of the umbilical cord. Sara and I felt very lost and alone, but still retained instant access to the Royal Marsden. We returned to a strange house, our home, but unlike anywhere we had ever lived before. You move from normal life into the alien world of children's cancer, but making the transition back again is also necessary. What do you do now? Despite the brief time span, we had become institutionalised and dependent on the hospital without even being aware of it. Our lives had revolved around a regime, which included a timetable for meals, ward rounds, giving drugs, and bedtimes. These developed into part of our daily routine as we geared ourselves to Unit living, and the fellow parents and patients grew into close friends. Fate had initially thrust us into this unfamiliar environment, and now we were abruptly leaving it. This loss of support can cause the collapse of your coping mechanisms. Gradually we readjusted and became a family again, but the overshadowing from Max's disease did not lead to a normal life.

Families often discussed their yearning for the end of therapy, and how much their lives would improve afterwards. It was their major goal, as it had been for us, but the reality was different. The hospital and other parents supply support during treatment, and there are immediate obstacles to overcome. Afterwards, we faced a grey cloudy goal of five years free of cancer that might signpost Max's long-term survival. Most people behaved as if the illness had ended and expected us to continue living normally. This is not true. Life continues but is never conventional because you watch and wait; constantly.

There are degrees of resulting concern depending on the case history and your knowledge of the disease. Sara and I were very aware of the problems relating to Max's potential relapse because they might be confused with non-specific symptoms of other illnesses. We had to define our boundaries. Temperatures were fine, provided they were associated with some visible explanation. We could cope with spots, a cough or cold, and anything ascribed to a specific cause. We knew Max like a finely inscribed map and had watched him in minute detail throughout his treatment. Sara and I had subconsciously catalogued every symptom and reaction. Temperament and morale fell into this category. Filed away were all those little signs one cannot put into words and which defy reason. Sometimes our observations made no sense, which caused worry as we raised the alarm.

When the Royal Marsden discharged Max, the doctors said his health would soon recover, and that the chemotherapy would have no lasting effect. This did not happen in our case. I have a photograph of him taken a couple of months after returning from the hospital, which showed him as a bundle of skin and bone. Having scooped him up in my arms and cuddled him, he was tiny and weightless, and I remember thinking "What has happened to my child?" I wanted to hold him forever. Those precious moments and snapshots you want to relive repeatedly; yet all that persists is the celluloid.

Max suffered from aches, pains, and weakness after his leukaemia treatment ended. It was many months before he could walk more than a hundred metres without collapsing with exhaustion, and I carried him on my back when this occurred. We sometimes received audible caustic asides from passers-by commenting that he should be walking. I withheld my anger at these judgemental comments for the sake of Max's dignity. His inability to lead a normal existence continued, but five months later he kept complaining of feeling sick, started retching for no reason, and vomited twice. Increasing fatigue and worsening pains in his left leg compounded these symptoms and worried us immensely. He did not have a fever or local inflammation, and we had no idea what caused these problems. We had been down this road before, and a few of these indicators were comparable to those displayed prior to his leukaemia diagnosis. We took Max to the Marsden, fearing relapse, but tests declared him free of cancer, and we continued being cautious.

The second set of inexplicable warning signs occurred after we returned from a holiday, when Max had a fever but no other symptoms. Sara and I remained prudent, and we summoned the on-call doctor instead of overreacting and contacting the Royal Marsden. After we explained the complexities of Max's condition, the doctor referred us to the local hospital after admitting she knew little about childhood cancer. This scenario occurred twice, and I respect doctors who divulged their lack of knowledge but were prepared to listen to our concerns.

I took Max into the local hospital and the doctor isolated him straightaway before taking blood tests. The nurses were excellent, and a few had been on duty during his first admission. They inserted a temporary intravenous line into his arm, and he picked up during the day after receiving medication to reduce his temperature. I had doubts again and wondered if I had overreacted, but the lack of an immediate definitive answer from the doctors put those thoughts to the back of my mind. Again, I lay awake drinking coffee through the night until I received the blood results. They were normal. Dr Solomon, Max's first consultant, saw us the following morning and yet again showed consideration and care. He could not make a diagnosis but suspected a viral illness, despite not having any direct evidence for this conclusion. The temperature had subsided, and Max's blood counts were normal, so the doctor ushered us out with the highest priority.

All was well.

Max

Chapter 7

It is difficult describing the quirks and qualities of offspring to strangers, because your children are very special, despite not being perfect by any degree. The narrative interleaves plain description with years of love and time spent as a parent, but does not convey every emotion, especially if your child has died.

After confirmation of Sara's pregnancy, we deliberated over names for our first child. Max or Maxine were our favourite options, and we unofficially christened the baby long before the birth. The unborn child was active in the womb, and a friend nicknamed it Wrigglesworth while commenting on the movement of the foetus. However, we never used this as a middle name because we thought it cruel to burden him so.

Max's due date was 08.08.88 but he was three days overdue, which disappointed us because we believed such a run of numbers was auspicious. Two and a half years after his death, a similar coincidental sequence with the number eleven occurred during the solar eclipse. On what would have been his eleventh birthday, at eleven minutes past eleven, an ominous shadow swept across the landscape; birds fell silent, animals stopped grazing and stood still as an icy wall of darkness engulfed us. As the moon blocked out the sun, I found this moment strange, poignant, and very moving.

Sara's labour lasted ten hours, and the nurses eased the baby into the world with forceps. I stayed with her throughout the birth and watching my wife go through so much pain left me with an enormous respect for the toil women undergo during delivery. The child's gender did not bother me, my only minor reservation was an aversion to auburn hair. Exhausted, Sara smiled as she took Max into her arms before shrieking weakly with laughter, "He's got red hair, he's got red hair!" Having seen blood on his head, I assumed this caused the reddish hue, but then laughed at her delight and my discomfort on seeing his ginger fuzz. My real concern lay with the health of my son and Sara's survival. After the doctor declared our baby healthy, we let out a sigh of relief.

Life became difficult after Max's birth, as is common for lots of parents, and we found his severe colic and erratic sleep patterns distressing and very tiring. Many illnesses throughout his early months also worsened this strain.

Max grew into a toddler, and like other young children had a fascination with anything loud and mechanical. When we lived in rural Wales, he yelped with joy on seeing a tractor or muck spreader. His favourite vehicles were combine-harvesters because their sheer size and noise left him in awe. After we moved to the city, he became entranced by motorbikes because of the racket they made when passing.

Two occasions before Max's illness caused us to think hard about the vulnerability of our child, and the first occurred while moving to another house. Normally we were very conscious of his whereabouts and actions, realising a second's lapse can be at your peril. I had replaced the child gate at the top of the stairs with a mattress to stop Max passing as we moved furniture down to a van. I heard a thud, thud, thud as something heavy fell. The repetition confused me, because if Sara had dropped anything there would have only been a single bump as it hit the ground. I grasped what had happened as she shrieked with horror, and we discovered that Max had pushed the mattress out of the way and fallen down the entire flight. As he lay motionless and momentarily silent, we were sick to our stomachs and could not believe what we saw. He then screamed, reassuring us he was still alive.

We rushed Max to the local hospital where the doctor diagnosed a bruised ankle but nothing more. Halfway through the visit, I realised that the staff were scrutinising us in detail because they suspected mistreatment of our son. I was ashamed that my actions had resulted in his injury but respected the fact the nurses needed to know whether it was accidental.

The second occasion our lives appeared threatened by the loss of Max occurred in a large open plan furniture store. Sara and I separately wandered around various parts of the shop as he ran between us. After saying he was going to see his mum, she approached me a few minutes later and asked where he had gone. We scanned the warehouse floor but could not find him anywhere, and our concrete reality turned to dust. I questioned people near the sole exit to see if anyone had left with a red-haired child, but to no avail. Despite warning our three-year-old about talking to strangers, he was too young to understand. We searched and desperately called him. After five minutes he crawled out from the inside of a carpet roll, thinking his disappearing act had been a great wheeze. He received a strong reprimand from us both. Overwhelmed with relief, we could not believe our luck that Max remained unharmed. These are the minor incidents befalling many families in the difficult yet rewarding task of having children, but we could never have foreseen what was to follow.

When Max was a toddler, we played what he called the Vidian Armchair game when sharing a bath together. The name originated from a mispronunciation of the word video, combined with the armchair from the children's program "Jim'll Fix It." It had lots of buttons which triggered events in the show. My knees represented the arm rests as he leant against them and pressed imaginary buttons, waiting for the outcome with eager anticipation. In response, I uttered a strange noise or made a manic movement such as shaking an arm or leg. The climax resulted when I dropped my legs and he slid into the water with shrieks and peals of laughter. This play was repetitive, as is common with young children, but it never lost its attraction. The giggles pouring forth with each new action were a joy to hear.

Despite being an alert, animated, and intelligent child, Max did not stand out at school because he was one of the youngest in his year. Science and natural history television programs were a specific fascination, and he was inquisitive and intrigued by the world around him. Max's other television passion, aged four, was the Power Rangers show. Sara and I had our reservations concerning these superheroes. However, we liked their catch phrase of "Believe in yourself", and often repeated it back to him as a confidence booster. This proved a useful motto in the following years and helped him cope with his illness.

Max suffered from bedwetting, and Sara and I worried this might signify physical or emotional problems. After seeking medical help, the doctors said neither of these were the cause. We persevered in trying to solve the issue, which resulted in sleepless nights and the endless changing of sheets. Although stopping just prior to his leukaemia, it returned after his diagnosis and continued for another two years. Max had difficulty sleeping and often cried out at night that he was afraid or had experienced a nightmare. I stroked his forehead, as my father had also done when I could not fall asleep.

As a toddler, Max had a fierce imagination that gave rise to his two imaginary friends called Jack and "Bear Me." Jack always took the blame for Max's indiscretions, such as spilling milk or breaking a cup, but I cannot remember much about the latter character. Sara and I loved listening to his conversations with these make-believe playmates and indulged him in his fantasy. He was also a sensitive child, as shown by comments on the softness of someone's skin, or on the beauty of a feather and the colours in the sky. He had a tactile sensitivity uncommon in boys and was also caring and thoughtful.

Max had a deep-seated fear of wolves and lions, and neither Sara nor I ever discovered the origin of these anxieties. They embodied his consternations; the Lion prowled in dark rooms, and attacks by wolves developed into an excuse for avoiding other upsetting scenarios. I remember taking him for a walk in West Wales, and he told me that the Lion lived in the cave we could see in the distance. After growling at the cavern as he emulated the beast, he burst into tears because he had frightened himself so much. I cuddled him and as he quietened, he told me that the Lion's snarling had frightened him. Max was a shy child and on starting nursery school sometimes felt intimidated by the other children.

This resulted in the unfortunate response of him growling like a wolf, and them crying and running away.

I loved indulging Max's imagination when he was five years old, and we concocted stories during his bath times. My hands represented two of the heroes, which I called the Crawling Crab and the Dancing Lobster. Max had a plastic penguin, christened Peter, and we added many other toys and pretend people into the narratives. These chats about their lives often turned into intricate tales. I likewise encouraged him to invent characters at bedtime and then strung them into a fantastic fairy-tale. It included Crab Burglars, Wicked Dinosaurs, or creatures imagined on the spur of the moment. At first confused, he was later delighted on realising he could determine the storylines. This always lasted for around half an hour before I drew the session to a close and agreed to continue the following night.

Within our family there were many times where either Sara or I unexpectedly said the same sentence simultaneously with Max or Paula. Both loved and were in wonder at these quirks and shouted "Twins" when it occurred. This developed into a game, where we as parents vied with our children for the honour of being the first to shout our recognition of these coincidences.

Before Max's illness, Sara and I limited his video game playing because we thought it was a waste of his time. This view changed during his leukaemia, and the game "Sonic the Hedgehog" gave him a focus and immense satisfaction as his skills improved. He often challenged us to a game of Sonic and our lack of coordination amused him immensely, as did the fact that he could thrash us in any contest. The game became a talking point with his peers in the Unit, and as a competent five-year-old player he sat dispensing advice to far older children. This ability earned him respect and offered common ground with other unfamiliar patients. In later years, video games provided refuge from the world of childhood cancer and salvation from his deeply withdrawn moods.

Max, Paula, and I had many chase games. One was Bula-Bula, which evolved in West Wales while playing with their cousin Karen. I do not know the origin of the name, but the game entailed them shouting Bula-Bula at me as a taunt and me chasing them round an enormous garden. Another involved me as the evil Mister Pento prowling around Max and Paula's home base as they again taunted me until I pursued them. I hid, and it required considerable daring on their part to venture forth from their sanctuary without me catching them.

As a young child, Max loved dressing up and Sara had lots of costumes for him and Paula. On one video we have a scene of him and his best friend taking this to bizarre extremes, not because of the nature of the clothes but their use. Both boys stuffed the costumes up their loose tee shirts and into their baggy trousers, and after five minutes had become weird caricatures of themselves. With huge inflated chests and thighs like trees, they staggered around the room barely able to walk, roaring with laughter at the ridiculous scenario.

The Make-A-Wish Foundation provided us with a holiday at Disneyland in Florida a year after Max finished his leukaemia treatment, which we needed and thoroughly enjoyed. Max and I took the Splash Mountain ride during the trek round the theme park. This is a slow but enjoyable journey along a route in log boats, culminating in a fifty-foot steep descent into a pool of water. The forty-five-degree decline was exhilarating. Afterwards he told me how scared and excited he had been as his heart had gone boom-de-boom. We took the trip a second time, but as we approached the long fall, he panicked and said he could not face it again. As he climbed out of his seat, I became worried about how I would cope with my hysterical child during the culminating decline. I held onto Max to calm him, and he screamed as the boat plunged headlong into the pool below. After it stabilised, he turned and leered at me with a massive grin, "Hey Dad, fooled you then!" His wind-up incensed and delighted me but also relieved my concern.

It was important for Max to have a best friend during his time in the Unit. He found that friendship with James, who had an unidentified brain tumour. They became devoted to each other and showed a mutual care and concern that boosted them each time they were miserable. This bond helped us raise them from their hospital beds to get them running around like healthy little boys; wild, cheeky, and full of spirit. This indefinable essence helped them fight whatever lay around the corner and is comparable to the

Chinese concept of Chi. The power of your mind and body working in unison can sometimes achieve the apparently impossible, and we wanted to nurture this life force.

On one occasion I spent an hour chasing Max and James around the Unit, but they became overexcited, so we moved outside to the climbing frame. This was the first occasion they had been healthy enough to leave the wards to play in the fresh air and sun. We walked round the hospital grounds with James's mother and Sara later the following afternoon, and everyone enjoyed this outing. James and Max became such good friends that neither wanted to leave the hospital because they would miss each other so much.

I remember them both manically tearing around the Unit with an older friend from Max's leukaemia days. This mischievous child introduced the younger pair to the joy of syringes. After raiding the Dispensary for large unused empty hypodermics (without the needles), they filled them with water. Mayhem ensued for the next two hours as they squirted one another, the staff, and any parents they were confident enough to pester. I became their prime target but bowed out because of my inability to keep up with their frenetic pace, and they had also soaked me through to the skin. They continued running about, but the nurses put an end to the chaos because it interfered with the treatment of other children. If you had seen these three boys elsewhere without their balding heads, you might have assumed they were no different to any others as they played wildly together. Their energy was astonishing given their respective illnesses, and a case where fun and play showed its vital importance in the healing process. Eventually they collapsed, exhausted, but had thoroughly enjoyed themselves.

Aged seven, and long before his tumour, Max became obsessed with China. We as parents did not instigate this passion, and when asked the reason for his fascination he replied that he loved the differences between the Western and Chinese cultures. The writing, costume, mythology, and anything related to this magical civilisation thoroughly captivated him. During the Chinese New Year, just after his second diagnosis, we took Max to a restaurant which had advertised an outdoor performance of the Lion Dance. Despite Sara and I worrying that he might catch a cold, we waited in the bitter weather for the delayed troupe, but he refused to leave. The group arrived half an hour late, and the dancing left him entranced and enthralled. Later he posed for a picture in front of the Lion, and his face lit up with wonder and joy, vindicating our decision to stay.

During Max's tumour treatment, the nurses admitted a Chinese girl to our ward in the Children's Unit. Her mother was in a state of shock and her confusion grew when she looked at the area around his bed. It included a huge Chinese fan hanging from the wall, pictures of Chinese dragons, and oriental lanterns suspended from the lights. Max was desperate to meet the girl, but too shy to start a conversation. After the family settled in, I made the first move by showing the fan to the child, Li Ming. She and Max started talking and within two hours were in her bed happily filling in a colouring book while sharing his Easter eggs. Like an old couple, she chastised him and told him what to do; he retorted likewise. Those moments brought me much happiness and I would love to recapture them.

It was difficult watching the nurse question her parents while familiarising them with the ward as they clerked in Li Ming. Experiencing déjà vu, it brought back memories of our own first days at the hospital. The discomfort arose because her diagnosis of Acute Myeloid Leukaemia was the same cancer Max had suffered from three years earlier.

Doctors and nurses tried explaining the illness and its treatment to Li Ming's parents over the next two days. Particularly devastated, her father stared endlessly into the distance, trying to reconcile his former memories with the current desecration of his daughter. Her mother wanted to know what she had done wrong and whether lapses by her had resulted in the disease. I told her that no one knew the causes and she should not blame herself. Our earlier experience of this cancer helped my explanations, but Max's return with a tumour did not. Language problems led to difficulties in her interpretation of my answers, and likewise with my understanding of her questions. I had enormous sympathy for the overseas parents in the Unit, because often their English was sketchy to non-existent. In a foreign country and culture, far away from home, family, and friends, they were attempting to understand explanations hard to grasp even as a native English speaker.

Many months later, after Max's and Li Ming's treatments had ended, we were thrilled to hear she had a hospital appointment on the same day as us.

Max bought a silver locket and a bunch of flowers for her with his saved pocket money. Two days beforehand he said to me, "Daddy, I haven't been able to sleep for the last few nights, I'm just so excited and nervous about seeing Li Ming."

Sara and I were privileged to see him with his first love, especially poignant given his terminal prognosis.

I had a close relationship with Max long before his illness. As he grew older, we turned into a double act in which we made fun of each other, and I became the target for his taunts and barbed jokes. Prior to his second cancer I kept relatively fit by renovating our house and doing Kung Fu, but since then had gained weight. One day I made a throwaway comment in front of Max about my increasing waistline, and he latched onto it like a leech. Subsequently he laughingly referred to me as his "Fat Daddy", revelling in my resultant irritation.

I often reciprocated Max's teasing. In the early days of his second treatment, he became ill from the chemotherapy and often vomited. The nurses gave us a stock of disposable cardboard sick bowls for use at home, and he carried one everywhere in case he threw up. When travelling in the car it remained firmly wedged under his chin, but elsewhere he wore it as a hat, which he thought hilarious given its intended purpose. Max stopped being sick as the treatment progressed but refused to go anywhere without this comforter. I made fun of his reliance on the "Security Sick Bowl", which later turned into the abbreviation SSB. In the end he tired of my jibes about his unnecessary dependence and left it behind to prove he did not care.

Once Max got the hang of teasing and pranks, I became the butt of most of them. One example occurred while I chatted with my sister, when he walked into the kitchen and silently climbed up on the bench next to me. He peered into my ear and announced that someone had stolen my car. I looked round, alarmed that it was not in its usual parking space, but then spotted it in the corner of my vision. After telling Max that Sara must have moved it, I resumed my discussion. He continued peering into my ear before announcing he could see it, leaving me somewhat irritated.

"What are you doing, Max?"

"Looking at your car."

This strange behaviour confused me, but my sister roared with laughter because his comment implied my head was empty, and that he could see through to the other side. This resulted in him extending my nickname to "Fat Daddy with No Brain." Max loved goading me, because he knew I would chase him in return for his jibes, and this play often ended up with a tickle fight.

When Max was seven years old, we saw the film "Casper", which we both enjoyed. In this story, both a girl and her father move to a house haunted by three wicked ghosts and that of a child named Casper. The dad and daughter repeatedly made promises to one another, but special pledges resulted in a ritualistic linking of little fingers to seal their vow. Max adopted this convention with me, and it continued until his death. If either of us requested a Casper promise, we too linked our little fingers to signify an unbreakable contract. This became important in later medication battles, because if Max thought he was not capable of keeping the terms being set, then he refused and made a normal promise. If he took part in a Casper promise, it was absolute, sacrosanct, and never broken.

A similar ritual arose during Max's second cancer. Before his tumour we often watched television and cuddled on the sofa in the evening but could not do so after the illness. The pain caused sensitivity and the chemotherapy made him unnaturally hot. He blamed me for the latter, christening me with the new nickname of "Hot Daddy." We compromised by him curling one hand round my thumb, and this developed into our replacement for a cuddle. After Max's death, I spent many evenings on our sofa curling my hand around my thumb to comfort myself, and as a way of remembering our times together.

Lest I be too doting a parent, on occasions Max was exceedingly difficult. At times he had a temper and wearing stubbornness that later served him well as he fought his cancers. More than anything, I remember Max for his courage, gentleness, and humour, and for the love, laughter, and close friendship he freely gave and allowed me to reciprocate.

Allan

Chapter 8

was born in Wales and lived with my family in the countryside on the outskirts of Cardiff. My father became a decorated Squadron Leader aged twenty-three and was a modest, successful businessman who ran several companies. My mother was a housewife who looked after me and my two sisters.

Our house had a large garden next to both a wood and decrepit mansion containing a scrapyard. My parents raised chickens after the Second World War, and the garden surrounded two large unused poultry sheds. All these were exciting for a young child. My friends were children from the local primary school, as well as my cousins who lived half a mile away.

My mother described me as being a strange child, possibly because of my imaginary friend, Aggeston, who accompanied me everywhere during my adventures in our garden. I was headstrong, difficult, and had many quirks. I refused to eat the curved half of a piece of toast and often removed all my clothes after my mum dressed me, before stubbornly dressing myself again. This willfulness caused problems with my discipline. If sent to my bedroom with no tea, then I refused to come out or even eat until someone pleaded for me to do so. I preferred to suffer than capitulate, much to the chagrin of my unfortunate parents.

I performed well at school and remember my primary teacher approaching my mother.

"Hello Mrs. Buchanan, I'd like to have a quick chat about your son."

"Oh dear, what's the problem."

"Nothing, I just wanted to say what a pleasure it is to teach him. He's so well behaved and is exceptional in his schoolwork."

"I think you're talking to the wrong mother; you realise that my son is Allan?"

"Yes, the little boy playing over there."

My confused mother asked me why I was a model child at school but was so difficult at home. I had no adequate explanation.

We spent our holidays in a village nestled into the West Wales coast. We moved there when I was thirteen after my father bought an old Manor house, which he spent renovating over the next ten years. Meanwhile, I transitioned to a public school and into a fast stream class that took exams a year before the other children.

Unlike many public schools, the regime was friendly, but I felt very homesick during my first year. I was not particularly rebellious, though sneaked out with friends to local pubs or the cider farm. I joined Venture Scouts while there and learned scuba diving, which I continued to do on my return home during the holidays.

My breaking of the rules never resulted in major punishment, though the Headmaster did once request my presence. I entered his study with apprehension, unsure of what misdemeanour could have triggered his demand.

"Sir, you asked to see me?"

"Hello Buchanan. Yes, it's about your appearance. In all my time teaching, I have never seen such a scruffy student as you. Tidy yourself up."

"I'm not sure what you mean, Sir," I replied innocently.

"Tuck your shirt in, pull your trousers up, and what on earth has happened to your tie?"

"It was run over by a car."

"Are you trying to be funny?"

"No sir, it really was run over..., though not while I was wearing it," I added with a grin, which did not help matters.

"Well, sort yourself out and get a new tie."

"Yes sir."

I left his office proud to have created a memorable impression.

The only occasion I nearly ended up in deep trouble was when about twenty of us went to a large party on the Common about five miles away. Some culprits were day boarders, and the school could not discipline them for what they did in their free time. However, most were full boarders, and the teachers detected their absence during a random roll call that evening. I had booked an exeat (a valid temporary absence) and said that I was staying with my sister for the weekend.

The teachers had got wind of the mass exodus and appeared in force with a van to search for the missing students. Despite us breaking into small groups, word soon spread about the arrival of my Housemaster and the other teachers to round up the offenders. I spotted him striding towards me and dived underneath the school van, only to find myself next to another classmate. The teacher had not spotted me, but we were concerned that the van might move while we were under it. We managed to escape undetected, and my day boarder friend returned home. I hitched back to the school and slept inside a hollowed-out tree in a nearby field, having taken a sleeping bag for just such a scenario.

Pleased to have avoided the round-up, I awoke the following morning to discover that I was sleeping amongst myriad red spiders, beetles, and other insects. Disgusted, I removed what I could from my hair and returned to school, but on my arrival received instructions to see my Housemaster.

"Hello Allan, how was your exeat? Did you have a good day with your sister?"

"Yes, thank you sir."

"Did you visit her, as opposed to going to the party last night? Perhaps you can describe your day to me?"

I gave a brief description of a fictitious outing and the Housemaster smiled.

"Buchanan, you and I both know that you were at that party, but I have no way of proving it. I could ring your sister, but I suspect you've already briefed her. I didn't catch you this time, but I'll be watching you closely from now on."

However, after I finally left the school, I received a ban from ever going back, because I returned to visit friends who had stayed on for another year. We all snuck out for a drink, but on our return a teacher passed us on the stairs as we walked up to a friend's room.

"Hello Buchanan, I haven't seen you for a while, everything OK?"

"Yes sir"

We ran upstairs, and I hid in a cupboard. Two minutes later the teacher realised that I had left the school a year beforehand and returned to eject me from the premises. My parents received a letter stating that the school was prohibiting me from ever visiting again, which they and I found amusing.

When not at public school, I returned to our Manor House in West Wales, which was in a permanent state of renovation. It was a grand three-storey ancient building, which we all loved, but there was something creepy about it. I always ran from the ground floor to my bedroom on the top floor when alone in the house.

One day I saw five people standing outside pointing at my bedroom window, and my father went to investigate why. Amazingly, one was a cousin of his who was unaware we lived there, and Dad invited the family in for tea and a chat. During the conversation, a woman announced that a friendly spirit haunted my room. I discounted her talk as absurd, but later changed my mind. On one occasion I heard a thudding in my room ceiling in the middle of the night. I got up and tried to determine where the noise was originating from, intending to investigate its source the following day. I moved towards the noise in the corner, but it switched to another part of the room. Each time I tried to locate its source, it spookily moved away. When I eventually told my parents about this odd event, my mother announced that she too had once experienced strange occurrences with my room. She had come up late at night to tell me to turn my music down. Her annoyance turned to alarm on discovering me asleep and the stereo switched off, despite the faint sounds of music emanating from within. My father then upped the ante by saying he had seen a harmless apparition of a young girl in the adjoining corridor. He steadfastly maintained this story until his death thirty-five years later.

We had some unusual animal experiences while living at the Manor. Twice I woke to hear my mother screaming in abject fear because bats had escaped from the roof and were flying around my parent's bedroom. My mother, an avid bird watcher, rescued twenty-one Manx shearwaters and a young gannet that had washed up on the shoreline, battered by a storm. The shearwaters sat on our derelict middle lounge floor for five days as the rough weather abated. Afterwards we took them to a clifftop, and all flew off successfully.

We also rescued another gannet, but this was a more difficult visitor. It too washed ashore during a storm, but the poor weather was the least of its problems, because it only had one leg and eye. White adult gannets have a two-metre wingspan and survive by diving torpedo-like at up to sixty miles an hour to catch fish fifteen metres underwater. Our gannet was young, brown, and measured one and a half metres between its wingtips. On initial inspection one would think it incapable of doing much at all, but despite its disabilities; it was a formidable foe. We had a Jack Russel terrier and a Labrador, both of which viewed this damaged bird as an intruder and valid prey. They tried to attack the gannet, but it drove them away with its vicious beak and flapping wings, the latter being strong enough to break an arm. We let the gannet roam the front garden but curtailed that practice because it attacked the postman, who announced he would not deliver our mail if it was present. My parents gave me the task of feeding the bird, and I used to go fishing every couple of days for pollack to provide it with fresh food. Despite being its closest companion, it still used to attack me, so I left the fish at a safe distance. The bird became very smelly, so we took it to the beach to swim in the sea, which ended up in a complete farce. We let it loose, but it tried swimming for freedom with its one leg. My father chased it in a rowing boat, but he slipped and lost an oar, which then started floating out to sea. After the onlookers recovered from their laughter, I swam out and recovered the oar, my father, and the recalcitrant bird. Despite our best efforts, the gannet died a few weeks later after its eye and leg infections caused more serious illness.

Our middle lounge was the last room requiring completion but suffered from damp creeping up the corner wall. My dad cleared away the earth under the floorboards and discovered a ring of stones. We knew that a watercourse ran under the house and these looked like they might have formed the top of a well. He decided that it needed digging out to discover the source of the moisture, and the stones continued for a small distance underground. I avidly took up this challenge. For the next ten days I dug a one and a half metre diameter hole in the clay, only stopping when it was three metres deep and I had reached water. We then lined it with concrete, which resolved the issue.

I completed my schooling aged seventeen but did not do well in my A levels and my previous run of academic success ground to a halt. My public school recommended that I do another year and retake my exams aged eighteen. My parents agreed, but I had no intention of doing so, because I wanted to take a yearlong break from education. I did not return.

I and my close friend Jon had arranged a job working in the North Sea oilfields, but it fell through a few weeks before it was due to start. This resulted in me spending six months as an assistant in a local supermarket warehouse, which was not how I had envisioned my year off.

Jon and I applied for a grape picking job in the Champagne region in France. We enjoyed the two weeks of arduous work, which introduced us to other travellers and itinerant workers. Their curious and wild stories reinvigorated my enthusiasm for travel. After we finished our stint at the vineyard, we hitched a lift back to Paris. But on arriving at the Gare du Nord railway station that Saturday, we discovered that all the trains for the UK had already departed. According to the timetable, our next available train would leave early the following Monday morning. Somewhat despondent, we realised we would have to spend two nights out on the streets before making our way home. Exhausted, we wandered down to Pigalle, the red-light district, and lay on some benches and tried to sleep. Various odd people disturbed our sojourns, but we shooed them away, except for the last more determined stranger. He was in his early thirties, scruffy and had long hair. Although he approached us speaking French, he was ecstatic when he heard our English replies.

"Thank God for that, I've been waiting to hear an English voice for ages. Fancy coming for a pint?"

I was loath to engage with this stranger; named Bill. Jon, however, pointed out that together we were more than a match for him, so we had a drink in the nearest café and explained our predicament. Bill said he could possibly provide a room for the night with friends, which although dubious seemed far better than sleeping out at night in Paris. We followed him into the metro but had to jump the barriers when he announced that he never paid. Our apprehension grew as he led us into derelict tenement buildings on the outskirts of the city. After a short and nervous wait, a group of French students turned up and started cooking a meal over a portable camping stove. They were an amazing bunch, accepted us without question and we and they shared what food we had. They could not provide us with a bed for the night, so Bill, Jon and I travelled elsewhere in Paris to see a woman who might have spare accommodation. She too could not help us, much to my relief because of the syringes littering her bathroom. We eventually spent the night sleeping on the floor in a flat of another of Bill's friends.

We said goodbye to Bill the following Sunday morning. Beforehand, he alarmingly divulged that both the UK police and Interpol had a warrant for his arrest. He had stolen a quad bike while on LSD and fled the country after escaping from custody. But as far as Jon and I were concerned, he had been a good friend helping us in our time of need.

We decided we would spend the night sleeping outside the Gare du Nord station, but became alarmed on discovering a trail of blood outside. Concerned, we followed it for about a hundred metres, but relented when we realised it led into dangerous back alleys. We sat down outside the station, along with about thirty desperate vagrants. Most were drinking alcohol, looked aggressive, and the pervading smell of homelessness was overwhelming. Jon and I slept in shifts to prevent a mugging, but kept nodding off during our watches. Relieved when the station opened at six o'clock the next morning, we moved inside in the hope of more safety.

I needed to visit the Gents, and an old crone in her sixties or seventies started shouting at me in French as I crossed the huge foyer. This resulted in considerable amusement for the rail staff, and I questioned a ticket inspector on why this tirade was so funny. He told me that the woman was an old whore who was detailing her sexual intentions if she managed to lure me home. I countered her hectoring with some good old English epithets and continued to the toilets in the basement.

Having relieved myself, two burly men came down the steps into the room and approached me with intent. Very rattled, I realised that there were few people on the concourse and that Jon would not hear any calls for help. The suited man held something in his hand and spoke forcefully, and I assumed he was trying to sell me drugs.

"Sorry, mate, but I don't understand you. I'm not interested."

"I think there's some confusion; we are the narcotics police. Please show us your papers and empty your pockets."

At this point I realised that he was holding a police identification badge. Mollified, I retrieved my passport from deep in my jacket lining. He inspected it, satisfied that I had valid documentation. I emptied the eight pockets of my camouflage jacket and handed him a toothbrush, toothpaste, comb, sun cream, and other innocuous items. He asked what I had been doing in France, and I told him we had been grape picking, and he appeared amused as he handed back my possessions. His expression suddenly changed.

"What's that in your top right-hand trouser pocket? Pull it out slowly."

I removed the curved grape picking knife with thumb and forefinger and both men tensed.

"Why are you carrying a knife? Do you realise that is an offence here in France?"

"I'm seventeen, have never travelled before and had to sleep outside the station last night. It's for self-defence," I replied contritely.

The two men started a deep discussion in French, as I contemplated explaining a foreign court case to my parents. The police radio activated, and with a flurry he announced they had to leave, but that he was confiscating the weapon and I handed it over with great relief.

I returned home, but wanted to continue my travels, and so applied to work in an Israeli kibbutz. Having journeyed to France by ferry, this was the first time I had flown, but there were significant delays at Heathrow. The risks of high jacking had resulted in extensive security checks by the El Al staff. While waiting, a call over the loudspeakers summoned me, and I had to go through a rigorous interrogation and search. This was not surprising given that I was again wearing an army camouflage jacket and all my belongings were in an army kit bag. The flight too was eventful; a man had a heart attack in the aisle and one engine failed before we landed.

I enjoyed my time on the kibbutz, and worked harvesting bananas, grapefruit, and avocados, together with working in the kitchens. I spent my free time with the other foreign workers, which involved frequent partying. This stopped after Israel invaded Lebanon, and the kibbutz warned us that we might have to retire to shelters if we heard gunfire or the rumbling of tanks. The Israeli air force performed practice strafing runs while we worked in the fields. It terrified us because we only became aware of the jet after it had roared past twenty-five metres above our heads. In modern warfare you often have little or no idea about impending attacks from the air until after the event.

I travelled to Greece from Israel but became ill and could not walk any distance. After a week I obtained medication from a pharmacy close to the bedsit but was shocked when I discovered that its normal use was for pre-operational sterilisation of the gut. It worked. Having recovered, I did not have enough money to return home to the UK and so looked for a job. I walked round Athens asking local businesses for casual employment, and two establishments said they would take me on. The first, a café on Syntagma Square and part of a major hotel chain, appeared the best option, and I worked there for a month. The second I later learned was a brothel!

My last letter to my parents had mentioned the Israeli war, but they had not heard from me for six weeks. I returned from a Greek island to Heathrow bus station for the paltry sum of £14. This involved a deal with a counterfeit watch and airline ticket that expired within the following twelve hours. On arriving at Heathrow, I hitched my way back to West Wales and arrived at the hotel run by my father and his partner, Dick. He pointed out that my parents were coming for their marriage anniversary meal that evening and had a suggestion. Rather than ringing them to pick me up, I should appear as a surprise waiter when they ordered their desserts. It sounded like a great idea, but almost went horribly wrong. I duly waited and followed Dick into the lounge with the tray of desserts. He turned to my father.

"Simon, I forgot to mention that I've taken on a new waiter and would like to introduce him to you."

I stepped forward with a big grin to hand over my parent's puddings. My mother let out a piercing scream, stood up, and started trembling. The dining room fell silent, and a man at the nearest table moved aggressively towards me to protect my mother. My father looked slightly alarmed, and uttered the incongruous comment, "Allan, what's wrong?" The entire episode had gone horribly awry, and Dick had to calm the dining room before leading my mother shaking to the bar.

"You little bugger, Allan. Never do that to me again because I nearly had a heart attack," she said as she hugged me, glad that I had returned safely.

After my travels, I joined the local inshore lifeboat and spent five years as a volunteer. Being a crew member was almost a rite of passage for the young men and women of the small village, and I am proud to have attended many call outs.

I eventually went to university to do a degree in Mining Engineering, and in my last year of the course had to work for a mining company. I travelled out to South Africa and had many adventures, but the working experience was disappointing. The platinum mine workers resented the foreign students and would not allow us to do anything meaningful while there. I wanted to experience drilling at the mine face but was told to sit on the pallets twenty metres away and have a smoke. Bored, I did so. While smoking a cigarette, my legs became entangled in what felt like wires, and so I pulled them to see what they were. Horrified, I discovered they were strings of fuse wire connected to detonators and that I was sitting on a ton of explosive. I extinguished the cigarette immediately. We later had some fun with fuses (without the detonators), which I and a friend pushed under a door of another colleagues' room before lighting them. He emerged coughing from the smoke, but we were unprepared for the deep gouges burned into the floor.

I returned from South Africa to continue my degree and started going out with Sara, who had been a close friend during the previous three years. Sara, however, brought the relationship to a close just before my final university exams, which had a significant impact on my results.

After leaving university with a Mining Engineering degree, I worked as an oil industry engineer in the Irish, Arctic and North Seas. I worked a two-week-on and two-week-off schedule and spent my spare time renovating a stone cottage in the village in West Wales.

Sara and I had a common circle of friends, but I avoided her and did not drink in the same pub or moved on if she arrived. Being a remote Welsh village, the pubs often stayed open to locals until early in the morning, and after that pub goers moved to other houses to continue partying.

Often people retreated to my almost derelict cottage for late night drinking, and on one occasion Sara turned up at the door with some friends to join the revelry. I ushered them in, uncomfortable by her presence, but did not want to cause a scene. The night progressed and became more raucous. During discussions about my cottage chimney, someone disagreed that it was big enough for anyone to stand in. Determined to prove otherwise, I climbed into the fireplace with my head well up the stack to show it was possible. I spent a few minutes having discussions with the partygoers through a small hole in the wall before Sara's voice chirped, "The more interesting question is whether two people can stand in there?" The overwhelming consensus was that this was highly unlikely, so she struggled her way into the very confined space. Surprised by this unexpected turn of events, I exchanged a couple of sentences with Sara and then we started kissing. It took a short while before the rest of the party realised that we had stopped talking and they issued their roar of approval. Neither of us had ever envisaged that our relationship would restart this way.

Sara moved into the cottage with me and we lived in utter chaos. Downstairs contained minimal furniture, the kitchen had an earth floor, and I had stored several tons of building stone in the lounge. Upstairs enclosed a partial bedroom wall that we dismantled on a whim. The cottage became more habitable over time, though I had an interesting telephone conversation with the electricity supplier.

"Hello, I think there's a problem with the incoming mains supply."

"I suspect not, because most customer problems originate after the fuse box and that's not our responsibility."

"That's not true in this case. All the insulation has disappeared from your supply cable. If I touch the gable end of the house on a damp day, then I get an electric shock."

"We will have someone at the property within an hour. Please do not go anywhere near the end of the house."

Sara and I married a few years later, but I was made redundant after the collapse of the oil price in 1986. Max was born two years afterwards, and I had a varied set of roles during the intervening period.

In my first job I became self-employed doing assorted building and decorating work. I named the business HTSI, derived from my mother's teasing and reference to me as a High-Tech Scientific Idiot. This led to an awkward moment whilst registering the venture when asked to explain the abbreviation, but I said the choice was random and had no real meaning.

I thought my qualifications would enable me to apply for a professional job in Wales, but there were no suitable vacant roles. Playing safe, I applied for retraining. There were three courses available in the Job Centre; Optoelectronics, Computer Aided Design, and Microelectronics. Knowing nothing about any of them, I signed up for the latter because the field was expanding rapidly and most likely to result in future employment. Despite hoping this fall back would not be necessary, no opportunities arose, so I moved to Swansea to do a year in college. I enjoyed and completed the course with distinctions but realised this was not my vocation because I needed a more challenging role than being a technician. Using the more interesting aspects of the course, such as becoming involved in circuit design, would require at least another year of full-time education. I decided against this choice because I had already spent four years doing my degree.

The course included a module on software that sparked my interest, and so I followed this path. This aspiration was not easy. It took a further eighteen months and four hundred job applications before I started work as a trainee Systems Engineer with the software company Electronic Data Systems (EDS).

In the intervening period I worked on a fish farm. I enjoyed building the trout cages, and it turned out to be a dream job when it solely involved feeding the fish. Twice a day, dependent on the state of the tide within the estuary, I travelled ten miles on my motorbike and fed the trout before returning home. This enabled Sara and I to support ourselves and go out a couple of nights a week.

After the fish farm, I spent a year with a business researching and intending to raise gold and silver from sunken wrecks. A close friend, a secretary, and I were the actual employees, and a few unmet shady characters in the background supplied the finance. I never worked out whether the backers were serious or using it as a tax fraud. Nevertheless, my time working there was exciting and fun. It was Treasure Island in the twentieth century, and with so few prospects I used to dream about what we might salvage. We never recovered anything, despite having potentially found part of a wreck in the English Channel holding silver bars. I handed in my resignation one month before Max was born because I had not been paid my previous month's wages, and the company folded soon afterwards.

Fortunately, I received an employment offer in the software industry two months later. I moved to London immediately, having been given three days' notice before starting my job. Sara stayed in Wales with Max, supported by her parents who lived nearby, but we reunited once I had settled into my new role and managed to rent a flat.

Max, Cancer and Me

Chapter 9

How do you react to the news of your child's cancer? Initially you respond with anguish, followed by an attempt to cope with the challenges. Most manage, but how they get by differs considerably, and it is only when delving into the minutiae that the variations become clear. These depend on your character, beliefs, former world experience, and on your hopes and fears. You erect barriers hastily, shoddy but still effective, and shore them up with rickety scaffolding that swings and sways in the wind. These structures serve their purpose while you rummage for the bricks and mortar to build something sturdier. Sometimes even the subsequent stone structures are ineffective, because the foundations are inadequate, and no one guided you with any plans. Although I had various reactions to Max's cancers, I could never have predicted any of them accurately before his illness.

Throughout most of Max's leukaemia and at the beginning of the second cancer, I believed it was unlikely he would survive. My rationale was: "Accepting his death prepares me for the future, but if he survives, I'll have lost nothing by taking this stance." This premise has huge flaws but worked for me at the time. You reach out and grasp for any belief to carry you through the grim times. Max's survival was a too remote and fanciful notion, and so I discarded such thoughts as being beyond my current mindset. When I told others this perspective, I always received the same reaction; "You must be positive." Nobody, apart from Sara and the hospital, understood the complexities and hurdles Max needed to overcome before this was possible. Many other parents in the Unit likewise did not dare consider their child's long-term prospects.

After Max's second diagnosis, with its later complications and poor chances of survival, I realised I needed to help him fight his illness. This required the dismantling of my self-protective wall and going against my instinctive feelings, because if I lacked that faith then he would sense the lie immediately. These cancer children have had experiences we healthy adults cannot conceive and are wise beyond their years. Sometimes they make journeys to places that we cannot even imagine, and they learn and absorb. This transformation is alarming because they have visited death's door too many times for them to remain the innocent children they once were.

Changing my perspective on Max's cancer was difficult because it required abandoning my props, those mental crutches there to help me hobble through this horror. I dropped my defences on behalf of my son, knowing that doing so left me psychologically exposed. In taking this decision, I realised that if he died then I would pay in spades. This was a perceptive thought given the consequences in the period after his death.

Being a parent of a child with cancer is exceptionally stressful, and I had experienced extreme pressure previously within a major project at work. This lasted many years and involved long days, impossible deadlines, and steep learning curves. This sink or swim mentality was known as a Death March, because of the demands placed on those involved. I worked hard and kept my head above water. Only once did I experience any effects of stress, which occurred when I became dizzy before returning home disoriented and hallucinating. The doctor said a virus might have caused these symptoms, but after describing my job he recommended that I work fewer hours to restore my health. In retrospect, I discounted the viral explanation because I had similar but less severe symptoms twice in the following year, but which disappeared after scaling back my time.

I coped well during Max's leukaemia and those around me reflected this assessment, but my body reacted differently. The sublimation of emotions was easy, but the building pressure needs venting. The effects of stress manifested themselves when we returned home on conclusion of the treatment. When I got up in the morning, my left leg often gave way and resulted in me collapsing on the floor in pain. The aching subsided after roughly five minutes and there were never any further symptoms during the day. Night sweats complemented these strange events, and I awoke to find the bedsheets soaked with perspiration even though I had slept well. I did not give this sweating a second thought, because apart from being inconvenient and unpleasant, it did not seem related to any health issue. The significance only became clear many years later when investigating extreme stress. Despite my concerns about these incidents, I did not visit my local doctor because I worried that she might dismiss me as a hysterical parent because of Max's cancer.

These symptoms continued for many weeks and occurred on an almost daily basis before I considered it necessary to take any action. I applied for a company medical which involved a general health check, in the hope an independent physician would perform an unbiased appraisal. After examining me, he said categorically nothing was wrong with my leg. Puzzled, he read back through the forms I had completed before the consultation. I had mentioned Max's leukaemia, and the doctor asked me whether he had suffered with problems with his left leg. After I replied that this was the case, he told me again that I was healthy and suggested the causes were psychosomatic. I accepted his verdict and my leg never buckled again. Many other physical problems arose after both Max's tumour and death, which took time to resolve and stress played a role on these occasions too.

Parents often feel guilty that they could have done more to get an earlier diagnosis. Max's tumour caused remorse after I noticed his raised perineum two months prior to the Rhabdo diagnosis, but before any other symptoms became obvious. After examining myself, I wondered whether a change of body shape in puberty caused the difference between us. The possibility of a tumour did momentarily cross my mind, but I was always looking for leukaemia. Dismissing this oddity, I reined in any wild notions to preserve my sanity.

I had self-reproach for a while after Max's tumour diagnosis and thought, "If only I had said something." With most cancers it makes no difference because if a child has the disease and it has not spread, then early or late diagnosis is not significant. Not so for aggressive or metastasising cancers. Might our lives have been different with an earlier diagnosis? In hindsight, the later knowledge that Max may have suffered from another and different cancer meant such contemplation was meaningless.

A further event that caused guilt was unrelated to Max, but instead concerned the deaths of other children with his disease. I sometimes thought, "One more child has died, so maybe that gives us a better chance of Max surviving." These sad reflections have no scientific basis whatsoever but are gut reactions and forlorn hopes you scavenge from the void to help you keep going. The death of a child with an identical cancer plays no part in the survival of your own. Each disease is independent and has no relationship to other children's illnesses. Human nature falsely views statistics in this way. It seems intuitive only a limited number of patients with a specific cancer can die within a given period, and this suggests a lesser chance of losing your child. This is not true.

Once Max's second cancer therapy began, my reactions to the illness changed as I accepted its reality. In many respects our lives had become easier than in the intervening years, during which we contemplated the horror of a relapse. Max's potential death was incomprehensible, so I stopped thinking about it and instead developed a peace and internal quietness.

This outward stability shattered two months later as I watched television at home, alone and late at night. A funeral scene appeared on the screen, and I fell apart while sobbing repeatedly, "I don't want him to die." This experience frightened me. Having had no inkling these simmering emotions lay beneath the surface, I realised this small release suggested the pain awaiting in the future.

A parcel and troubling letter arrived a month after this incident, having signed up three years earlier as a potential bone marrow donor with the Anthony Nolan Trust. The letter was a call for Stage Two testing, which occurs when your blood meets specific criteria required by the prospective patient. Having spent time during Max's treatment wondering how I would react if called to donate, the delivery of the testing kit upset me. It shattered my calm because I felt that the donation would be emotionally disturbing, and I was unsure if I could cope.

Many people worry about the general anaesthetic aspect of donation, but any concern by me seemed unreasonable because Max had undergone ten operations requiring full anaesthesia. My major fear was the clashing of the procedure with the end of Max's tumour treatment, which would be a tough time for us all. Despite these reservations, a marrow contribution might help save a life and restore some of the crazy imbalances in my world. There were other complications. What if I had a genetic factor that triggered a further cancer? I turned to the Professor for guidance, and he recommended I proceed unless the recipient had a specific disease. The probability of me having matching antibodies was around one in a hundred, but my blood samples were not a close enough fit for donation.

Despite coping with daily events, there were times when I just wanted to admit defeat and announce that enough was enough. One occurred when I took Max to Outpatients for blood tests, but an issue in the clinic had caused delays. We went to the Unit schoolroom where he drew for a while before becoming bored, and so we returned to the waiting room. A single mother I knew well sat next to me with a lost and distant look. Seeing her there surprised me because her son had completed his treatment the previous week.

"Is everything okay? Are you here for an appointment?"

She turned to me, distraught, and with tears in her eyes.

She whispered, "It's back."

Looking at her blankly, I had no idea what she meant.

"Johnnie's got leukaemia again and the Marsden can't treat him anymore. He doesn't know, and we're here so they can tell him. I just don't believe it because he looks so well."

The boy had been rushing around the Unit only a fortnight earlier, looking better than at any time throughout his long and difficult leukaemia treatment. This shocking revelation stunned me. I replied consolingly and said she could call us, and we would do anything to help. Inadequate and sorrowful, I held her hand but was at a loss what else to do. After she left Outpatients, I waited with Max for his forthcoming blood test.

James, Max's best mate from the hospital, appeared with his mum and a family friend. They had been waiting hours for a scan, but the scanner was not working. After I commented that this must be the last straw, James's mother stood and walked off in tears. I turned questioningly towards her friend, who dropped the bombshell that his father had suffered a heart attack the previous evening.

These two incidents left me devastated. I wanted to walk out and go to a beach late at night with a fierce wind blowing and the waves crashing. Desperately seeking the freedom to escape the confinement of this disease, I needed to announce, "Hey Cancer, that's me finished, you've won." Easy if this was my illness, but that was not the case. I could not opt out because I had to care for my family during this nightmare.

As we moved through treatment, I grew closer and closer to Max and my parental scanner became finely tuned. At times we were almost telepathic. At home, sometimes I thought I heard him calling at night, but on rushing to his bedside downstairs he said, "Daddy, I was just going to call you." Likewise, this strange scenario happened once when Sara was still trying to get to sleep. I awoke and said I had heard him crying out for us, but she replied that she had been listening and heard nothing. Deciding to investigate nonetheless, only on entering his room was I conscious of him whispering my name.

Nearly six months after his tumour diagnosis, Max spent his first night away from us and stayed with a friend. When picking him up the next morning, he ran into my arms saying how much he had missed me. Later he said he had dreamt that he was crying and prayed that I would come to his aid during the night. I had become agitated by his absence too and needed to cuddle him on his return. We were becoming utterly reliant on one another, and this interdependency worried me. My support helped Max fight his illness but resulted in a trade-off. I realised that giving total love while hoping to save my son's life also risked leaving me defenceless if he died.

Late one evening, when I was sitting in our kitchen, Max walked in silently and stood in front of me.

"Are you okay?"

He nodded.

"Have you had another nightmare?"

He shook his head. I questioned him further and he shook or nodded, but at no point spoke, which I found disturbing.

"Do you want a cuddle?"

He nodded. I kissed his bald head and we cuddled for ten minutes without talking. He just needed more love.

On the conclusion of Max's second treatment, I had spent many months looking after him and was indebted to my employer, but I had to consider going back to work. I told Max, and later that night he confessed his fears.

"Dad, I'm scared."

"What's causing that, Maxie?"

"I'm frightened of the dark."

"Are you sure it's not because of the illness or your treatment?"

"No, I've suffered much worse than this."

"Well, how do you feel about them?"

"There's one good thing and lots of horrible things. It's good having you around, but I hate being sick, having a Hickman Line and giving blood, being on drips, and feeling miserable. Dad, I don't want you to return to work. How will I cope if you're not here?"

"I have to work Maxie, so we can afford to eat and pay for the house. The only reason I've not gone back is because you've been so sick."

"If I became ill again, would that mean you could stop work?"

My blood ran cold, and the implications of this question horrified me. I had spent so long trying to give Max the will to fight. Now I faced the spectre of him willing himself back into illness just to keep me by his side.

"Maxie, you mustn't be ill. Surely it's not worth going through chemo, the medicines and all that pain again. None of that's worth having me at home."

"I'm not sure." He paused and then nodded. "Actually, it is."

Max's reply left me deeply sad because he had gauged his relationship with me against all that despair. This exchange caused me hours and hours of tears on many occasions after he died. It took years to reconcile myself with this statement, because he had quantified his love for me against suffering that I had watched but could not comprehend.

Max's understanding of the implications of his cancers revealed itself slowly, and he tentatively broached the subject.

"Dad, Dad, I think I'm dying."

"Now why do you believe that? What a strange thing to say."

"Oh, it doesn't matter."

"Do you often think about dying?"

"No, not really."

We were circling and skirting the issue. He was testing to see if I revealed the possibility of his death, and I was trying to protect him from this knowledge. This scenario occurred another couple of times, but at that stage I was not ready to confront the subject. I was unprepared for these sudden vital questions during his recovery from Rhabdo.

Max and I often watched films together, and after his second treatment we saw "Back to the Future." After the film ended, he said that he sometimes thought about the time ahead, so I cautiously asked what he expected.

"I think I'll be dead."

I was glad he had started to face his fears and talk about his prospects.

"Dad, what would've happened if I'd done something different or if I hadn't gone somewhere? Would that change everything and mean I wouldn't have got cancer?"

After explaining that every event determined the future, I said he was not responsible and neither we nor the doctors knew what had triggered his illnesses. These were his first overt contemplations. He understood that the treatment could kill, and I suspected he now realised the disease could be fatal too.

I wanted to contribute towards childhood cancer and tried helping other Unit families in several ways. I told them how the appliances in the kitchen worked, where to find fresh bed linen, comforted an upset child, or did anything else that eased their burden. We too had felt alone and lost in this unfamiliar environment. It was not nice.

Despite writing and offering empathetic support to three families outside the Unit who had cancer-stricken children, I received no response. However, I corresponded with another family for a year, and although we never met, they were grateful for my letters. I also helped two families at the start of their children's illnesses by telling them our reactions and showing them that everything they thought was normal under the circumstances.

I wanted to support another bereaved family after Max died, but this tragedy did not involve cancer. They lost their son five days after machinery ripped his arm off in an appalling farm accident. I vaguely knew the father and had drunk with him in the local pub years ago. Although I was going through tough times, I could not conceive the suffering they endured and told my sister I could supply solace if required. She recommended not because I was barely keeping my own body and soul together, an inappropriate time to try helping people in even worse circumstances.

Anger

Chapter 10

Anger is common within cancer and experienced by children and parents alike. This wrath is often a declaration of withheld pent-up emotions and can appear unexpectedly.

A seven-year-old boy had recently returned from surgery and was recovering from the anaesthetic, which causes patients to become confused and disoriented. Two nurses comforted him as he regained consciousness, but he confronted them with a violent and sobbing rage.

"It hurts."

"Where does it hurt?"

"Everywhere."

"The hurt won't last long. Just try to relax and you'll start to get better."

"Why don't you go away and leave me alone?"

"Please calm down. Do you want something to eat or drink?"

The child screamed his reply, "I said 'Leave me alone.' I hate you both and all the other doctors and nurses. I want to tear down the walls of this hospital and smash it into the ground."

This scenario lasted for ten minutes, as the nurses tried to calm the ranting and angry child.

His father stood by. "What can I do to help, what do you want? Just tell me what you need, and I'll get it for you."

The child's rage and pain subsided; he stopped crying and calmly addressed his father while looking him in the eye. "Yes, Dad, there's something you can do for me," he said clearly.

"I want you to go to the kitchen."

The father interrupted, expecting a request only he could satisfy given the antagonism by his son towards the nurses.

"Can I get you a drink or biscuit?"

"No, bring me a knife, a very long sharp knife so I can stab myself over and over again and stop this pain. I hate everything and just want to die."

As his composure dissolved, the boy sobbed uncontrollably. The father was distraught and close to tears. The nurses looked visibly stunned, and the child's mother stood in the ward doorway crying.

This was me, Sara, and Max.

The anger Max experienced is common in children with cancer and stems from the fact it has stripped their innocent lives bare and to the core. This loss of control forces them to come to terms with examinations, deprivation, and the invasiveness of medical procedures. The gross injustice of the illness results in vomiting, incontinence, and betrayal by their sore little bodies. After moving from the comfort of home into a ward full of critical patients, they have had their emotional lives stolen after losing the stability of family, school, and friends. When not in hospital, outpatient visits continue this constant disruption as the disease shatters previously simple lives.

I found this process stressful as an adult and observer but did not have to undergo treatment. In identical circumstances I would have had similar or worse reactions. The anger is understandable and natural, but a young child with an intense rage is exceptionally distressing for a parent.

While waiting for the prognosis for his tumour, Max often withdrew into himself by listening to music or playing video games in his bedroom. He refused to acknowledge our presence and did not respond when we talked to him. Instead he sat still, staring at the game screen or vacantly into space, as he retreated into the deep recesses and tried coming to terms with his second cancer. This occurred for hours on end until he surfaced as his usual self again. Sara and I found it hard coping with Max during this period, because we worried our little boy was alone and struggling with the impossible. We desperately wanted to help him but fretted that our exclusion from his lost world meant that he held us in some way responsible.

Besides the descent into blank trances, there later followed a furious anger that erupted without warning or provocation. He exploded when I mentioned medicine or anything connected with his new cancer, and during these episodes he screamed, shouted, and became unmanageable. In many ways we were glad to see these outbursts, because they expressed the turmoil boiling inside and were a far healthier response than their silent predecessors.

Max started to talk about his feelings and said he did not want people going on and on about his illness. He told us he was often in pain and was likewise upset by the recent intravenous line. Ten days after he began his second treatment, I tried yet again to get Max to talk to me about his feelings. Desperately hitting a beanbag, he was trashing his room to vent confused emotions in one of many frenzied explosions of anger.

"Max, I hate seeing you angry when I try to make you take your medicines and it makes me sad when you become upset."

He carried on beating the beanbag.

"I bet you wish that was me, because of the horrible things I've made you do throughout your illnesses."

He paused. "Oh no, not you Daddy, you're so lovely."

I knew he detested my constant nagging to take pills or to let me clean his dressing, and I posed the question to draw out his resentment. I never imagined this response and had readied myself for a torrent of abuse but received a single sentence showing his appreciation for my efforts. My reaction to his reply was far harder than anticipated because you steel yourself for the expected.

The battles continued but to a lesser degree, except for one argument that stands out in my memory. After a sleepless night for both of us in the hospital, Max awoke and confronted me with an explosive tantrum. He screamed and bellowed because I had not fetched a drink. Tired and unable to take any more, I too became angry because of my failure to understand the reason for the flare up. Losing my temper, I shouted back that he had no right to treat me this way. Despite doing everything in my power to help him, he had repaid me with an outburst based on a non-existent request. We sat silent and fuming for two hours in his isolation room. I felt guilty about yelling at my sick son.

"Max, I'm very sorry I shouted at you."

No reply.

"You're furious with me because I didn't get you orange juice, but you never asked for any. We're exhausted because we had a sleepless night, which makes us grumpy. I'm trying to do everything I can for you, but I can't read your mind or do things I don't know about. We've been cross for a while, but we need to resolve our differences. I should never have shouted at you. Let's be friends again?"

"I thought I'd asked for the drink. I'm sorry too. Even though I got so angry, I still think you're lovely."

This was the dissolution of our father/son relationship and the start of one of equals, triggered by the fact both of us had apologised and backed down. It resulted in a new mutual respect that grew and grew.

Max's anger issues dissipated as his treatment progressed, but they returned sporadically and sometimes became a problem. It is natural at the beginning of a child's cancer to pander to the slightest whim because you want to do as much as possible for your sick child. But this can create issues. Max realised he had us at his beck and call and began treating Sara and me as slaves. This conduct did not help with Paula's behaviour. How could we expect her to behave normally when her brother did so differently? We set our boundaries and tried to lead a normal existence.

Five months after his tumour diagnosis, I asked Max to eat breakfast downstairs instead of in his bedroom, because we did not want him dictating our family life. He flew into a rage and started screaming and hitting objects, and so I walked away and let him vent his frustration and anger. I returned a couple of minutes later, gave him a cuddle, and we went to eat. We cuddled again afterwards and talked about his feelings regarding the treatment and illness. He felt better for the shouting but the constant moving between the hospital and our home bewildered him. He wanted the security of staying in one place and disliked the treks between the two. Watching and listening to this pathetic little wasted figure wrestling with emotions far beyond his years left me close to tears. How do you help a child manage with these thoughts and reactions when you yourself are only just coping with the same feelings?

Parental anger is a common reaction to your child's cancer. Its recipients can be doctors, your spouse, or anyone who invades the terrible privacy of your situation. I felt little compared to many parents I knew. My simmering feelings were mostly hidden but became unmistakable and frightening during Max's tumour treatment. This directionless and diffuse rage waited for a challenge, and a valid reason for me to release my frustration and distress. I needed a justification to enable the volcano to explode and an excuse for the expression of a blind and meaningless fury. Wanting to harm or even kill somebody, I yearned for someone to allow me to breach and do the unacceptable. To hurt and be hurt; to beat them into a pulp and to turn my turmoil into physical pain. Thankfully this never happened, but the anger smouldered beneath the surface and only erupted once, though did not result in violence.

We used to place a traffic cone outside our home so Sara could park after returning from dropping Paula off at school. One morning after she left, a man removed the bollard and parked beside our house as I watched from our bedroom window in my dressing gown. The young man was obviously late for work and I opened the window and shouted at him, but he retorted that he had every legal right to park there. I exploded with indignation. Swearing and cursing, I threatened him and his car with extreme violence. His casual departure made me even more incensed. I was unsure how to react, but despite reaching boiling point, I had no intention of carrying out my threats. Instead, I grabbed four roofing nails and placed one under each tyre deep inside the treads. Moving the vehicle in any direction would have resulted in a puncture. These actions were irresponsible and may have caused an accident, but I needed to vent my anger.

I went back to change Max's dressing and clean the entry site for his Hickman Line. While tending him, a police officer and parking warden knocked at the door. Sara opened it and panicked. "My husband is in there!" Max lay prone in the room next to our front door, and I diplomatically apologised and explained the strain caused by his cancer. The policeman was understanding and relieved, saying he expected to find someone caving in the car with a sledgehammer. After accepting my explanation, he walked round the offending automobile while inspecting it, and my threats had obviously upset the hapless owner. How could I explain the nails after my contrite excuses? Fortunately, the policeman did not spot them but left a note asking the owner not to park outside our house. I would not dream of taking those actions now, but extreme stress pushes you into strange places, ones you prefer not to have visited. I removed the tacks before the driver returned and we never saw him in our street again.

The parking warden was sympathetic and said the County Council could classify the space as reserved because of Max's disability. I requested a permit, but they had run out of money for that year.

Fighting Back
Chapter 11

Max's leukaemia left Sara and I feeling powerless because we lacked the wherewithal to help him fight his disease. He did not understand the significance of his cancer at the age of four and a half, but this changed after his second diagnosis when aged seven. The earlier powerful chemotherapy led to his partial understanding of the consequences of treatment and the seriousness of the disease. During his tumour care, we resolved to do anything to keep him alive. This may sound odd because we had provided as much love as we could muster during his leukaemia. Our decision differed because we wanted to take an active role beyond the daily nursing. We decided to teach him how to help himself battle his illness.

Like anger, depression is another emotion often experienced by children with cancer. In its extremes, this psychological response results in a stage where the disease and therapy have sapped the life from your child. The fun recedes, leaving a soulless body and distant shell. It is deeply disturbing seeing this metamorphosis triggered by the constant mental and physical onslaught of the treatment. Depression can also manifest itself in other diverse ways, which is especially true for toddlers lacking the ability to communicate their feelings. These cases occasionally result in the child regressing, which is a coping and defence mechanism and affected various young children within the Unit.

Max's regression began after his admission for leukaemia, and he curled up on his bed while sucking his thumb. Soon afterwards he stopped using normal language and substituted baby talk in his exchanges with us and the nurses. This infantile behaviour alarmed Sara and me, but the doctors explained that children often react this way to extreme stress. Whenever it occurred, we gave him more attention, cuddled him, and he slowly returned as our four-year-old son. Max only regressed twice during his second cancer treatment, and on these occasions as reactions to traumatic events.

The disease spread to Max's spine not long after his tumour diagnosis. Moaning with pain, he became miserable because he could not walk.

"How are you feeling?"

"I don't feel well. Do you remember Zordon in the Power Rangers movie?" he replied weakly. This fantasy character had lain in a glass mausoleum as his arch enemy drained away his life force.

"Yes, I remember."

"I've got no energy and I'm frightened that I might be dying."

Sara and I pointed out that Zordon had recovered, and afterwards she talked to Max about helping himself by being positive. Later I had a similar conversation with him.

"Maxie, I know you're a tough little boy. When your back hurts, you won't let Mum and me help and insist on sorting out your problems alone. We and the doctors need to support you in the fight against your illness, because it's cancer that's the enemy. You amaze me with how you cope. I don't think I could handle the things you've faced, but you always manage to pull through. Although you're very miserable now, telling us how you feel will improve your mood. I realise it's difficult and sometimes you become angry, but it helps to talk. If you find you can't walk, then you must just keep trying, and eventually you'll discover its possible. Try, try, and try again. The consultants worry that your spine will stiffen up, which might stop you from ever walking in the future. We can't make you do this; the determination needs to come from you. Use your anger to help yourself."

I carried on talking for a quarter of an hour, trying to give him the faith and confidence to combat his disease. He nodded but remained silent, leaving me exasperated because everything I had said appeared to have fallen on deaf ears.

Later that day, Max rewarded Sara and I for our efforts when he asked to get out of bed and tried to walk. The damage to his spine prevented any normal forms of movement, but his staggering signified progress. With a hand on each knee and his back almost parallel to the ground, he struggled forward, bent at ninety degrees like an arthritic old man. Despite the pain, throughout his attempts he repeatedly muttered, "I can, I will." This determination left us awe-inspired, and his smile showed his enormous sense of achievement even though he only took a few steps. I never cease to marvel at the inner strength of these children afflicted with cancer. Within days he walked, although not without difficulty.

Sara and I encouraged this novel approach. We persuaded Max to become an even more steadfast and cussed child to help him find the will to battle his disease. Max's outlook changed, and he exhibited traits typifying me as a youngster. These are not characteristics one should necessarily commend, and he developed the stubbornness and bloody-minded determination needed to fight his disease against whatever the odds. This was an independence and courage I had forgotten in myself.

Max awoke as a different person after his first attempt at walking and ate bacon and egg for breakfast, cracked jokes, and played tricks on me. We had discovered a powerful tool; give a child belief in himself and you can achieve wonders. Later he started playing computer games with other children and revelled in the attention as he displayed his skills. I retired to the Parent's Room to read and left him talking tactics with his latest friends. This was the first time during his second treatment he had not had either Sara or I at his side. Seeing him independent again made our hearts soar.

Max used his tenacity to help another child whose cancer had spread to his spine. The boy's father approached me and queried how Max had progressed so quickly from his stooped condition to almost normal walking. I asked Max if he was prepared to aid one of his friends again. He agreed, but I absented myself from their talk. Afterwards Max described his discussion with the boy, saying he had recounted my conversation.

"I told him that if you think it's impossible, but keep trying, then in the end you'll manage to walk."

The boy tried walking and did so with some semblance of normality during the next week.

A few days later, Max and two friends were playing football in the corridor, though this differed from the traditional version. There was no goal, despite him being the goalie. A "save" occurred at any point he deflected the ball with his wheelchair while holding the handles for support. All three children squealed and laughed at this simple game.

"That's the best fun I've had since being in hospital," he announced afterwards. I cannot describe how much joy these scenes produced, because despite their desperation they showed the adaptation of these children as they fight their illnesses.

Max started sketching soon after his second diagnosis, and this developed into an important outlet during his treatment. His first picture showed a plane going to Get Well Land, and he said it was full of Tender Loving Care. He had a good eye for proportion, a steady clear hand, and copied characters from comics to create his own stories. The drawing involved a therapeutic concentration that took him away from the here and now, and he derived enormous satisfaction from his work.

Sara had researched visualisation techniques that use mental imagery to help people fight their illness. These require a patient envisaging how the body is defeating the disease, in the hope the psychological benefits will stimulate the immune system. Since then, Psychoneuroimmunology has become a recognised discipline in treating many illnesses.

There were pictures on the walls in the Outpatient Unit explaining the role of blood cells in fighting cancer. These illustrations showed the red and white cells as smiling rounded blobs, and the illness as angry blue angular shapes. As the cartoon strip progressed, the friendly blobs overcame the nasty blue invaders. Sara suggested that Max sketch similar armies of blood cells overcoming his cancer. Believing a positive frame of mind could only be beneficial, we thought that expressing his feelings about the disease might be helpful.

Sara and Paula went back to Wales over the Easter break three months after Max's second diagnosis. Max said goodbye from his hospital bed, but her departure left him upset and unsure whether he could cope. As a treat, I bought him a Chinese meal and afterwards we cuddled.

"You're the best Daddy, and you and Mummy are the nicest people in the world. I wouldn't want anyone else as my Mum and Dad."

"We're so happy you and Paula are our children. I've got an idea; why don't you surprise Mum by doing your Army Drawings before she returns from her holiday?"

"Ooh yes, she'll love that, but you mustn't tell her. It'll be our secret for when she gets back."

Max did not draw any pictures before Sara and Paula's return, but ten days later our suggestions were fruitful. There were no beds available in the Marsden, so we were in a different hospital when he copied his version of the bicycle riding clowns which adorned the curtains. The two-page drawing portrayed the clowns killing grotesque one legged monsters with three heads, and each blood-covered face looked distraught. Another sketch showed a triumphant Sonic the Hedgehog smashing the ogres into pieces, with a speech bubble announcing, "I'm your worst nightmare!" This emphatic positive statement mitigated his graphic and disturbing imagery.

The effects of the drawings were dramatic and immediate. During our appointment the next day at the Royal Marsden, Max behaved as if someone had administered a massive dose of adrenaline. He ran around manically, chattering away and full of vitality. The Senior Staff Nurse commented to me. "What have you given Max? I've never seen him looking like this, not even when he was well." Many people repeated this sentiment independently over the coming weeks. He exuded a radiant and animated spirit. The vigour was not just in our mind's eye and his general outlook also became positive, leaving us vindicated by this progress.

By and large, Max's general wellbeing and reaction to the chemotherapy and infections significantly improved from this point onwards. When I asked him why he thought he had remained healthy for so long, he replied that it was because of the Army Drawings. Max had spent over twenty days without complications, and this was twice his earlier record. Sara and I had achieved our objective and pulled him from an awful morass of depression by changing his feelings about himself and his illness. Despite not altering the course of the disease, we had at least given him a better quality of life and could have done no more.

Even though Max began walking again, he had limited mobility. The chemotherapy stopped further crumbling of his vertebrae, but the existing damage and other side effects meant he could not walk any distance. He made his way around our home and did so admirably, but there was no question of him walking into town. The hospital recommended a wheelchair, and that we register him as disabled to enable easy parking. This declaration of disability had negligible impact and although many people might perceive this as a major step backwards, to us it mattered not one iota. We still lived in the transience of our hour by hour existence and knew he needed help with his quality of life. The delivery of his wheelchair brought relief because we had become prisoners in our own home since his inability to walk.

Sara and I wanted desperately to go out together as a family, but that was easier than it sounded. When Max was well enough, we took him into town in his wheelchair and enjoyed these brief trips. Leaving the house was a relief, because like the hospital it made us feel imprisoned and claustrophobic. But he became ever more lethargic and often lay on his bedroom floor, fed up and nauseous. Frequently we found him staring into space and yet again we thought we were losing him to realms we could not enter. We tried boosting his mood, but there were many thoughts that he could not or refused to express. We had no way of imagining his emotions.

Having so much free time without being able to use it seemed criminal. Whenever I queried whether he needed help, he just asked me to make him better. These replies left me helpless. As a father I considered it my duty to do anything and everything for my son, but I could not satisfy this single request. He was spiralling into depression again, despite the success of the chemotherapy in treating his tumour. We worried he might give up because he could see no gain, so I talked to him about his feelings.

"Maxie, you need to start fighting again. You're always upset and the moodier you get, the worse it becomes."

"I feel so ill. All I want is to lie here and be left alone."

"But the Chemo is making you better. The doctors say it's working, and even I can see things are improving. Haven't you noticed that the pain and itching have stopped, and the tumour has shrunk?"

He nodded.

"Why am I ill if the Chemo is working? I'm becoming so thin now and don't feel any better. I don't want people seeing me looking like this."

The chemotherapy had resulted in a 10% loss of Max's weight over four weeks, and he looked skeletal. Earlier in the week he had walked a hundred metres but now was too weak to even leave his bed.

"You're unwell because although the Chemo is destroying the tumour, it also affects the rest of your body. It's not the cancer, but the medication that's making you sick. I know that doesn't help much and I can't take away the sickness, but you are recovering. It's especially important you keep drinking, because it helps flush the Chemo through you. As far as looking thin goes, I don't think people will notice if you are wearing a thick jumper."

Max nodded morosely and said he would try to drink more. Later he started talking to Sara.

"Mum, I'm trying to get better. I prayed for myself because I thought it might help."

"Maxie, we've got people all over the world praying for you. Your and their prayers are helpful."

"No, their praying doesn't count, because they don't know what it's like to be me."

Sara had no adequate response to this statement.

A week later Max's mood improved, and he requested a takeaway Chinese meal. This demand signified a step forward, and Sara suggested that we have a family picnic in his bedroom. I laid out the rug while she prepared the main course and side dishes. Max started eating, but then vomited. We cleaned him and asked if he wanted to continue, and he said he did. He threw up again, so stopped eating. The rest of us finished our food as he chatted away, happy to have taken part in this strange little feast. Within the next two weeks he was unbelievably well. We went to a local park, and he walked half a mile before I had to carry him back. The pain had disappeared, but he still suffered from extreme tiredness.

Rhabdo

Chapter 12

The suddenness of Max's leukaemia diagnosis created its own shock, but long drawn out diagnoses are no less traumatic. In these instances, parents know something is amiss despite the non-specific symptoms, and the family doctor does not realise their significance. This is not necessarily through lack of knowledge, but due to insufficient exposure. How many instances of childhood cancer does the average doctor see? Few, if any, and the physician reassures the parents and is usually correct because the symptoms are unrelated to cancer. On rare occasions this continues for months before the final referral and diagnosis. I previously suspected these parents were not as traumatised as those experiencing a sudden onset of the disease, because they had subconsciously prepared themselves for a serious illness. I no longer believe that to be true. Protracted diagnoses have their own hurt, as we were to discover while awaiting the result of the investigation into Max's potential second cancer.

Sara became concerned by Max's complaints of itching and occasional pain in his perineum, which sits between the testes and the anus. Everyone informed did not regard his symptoms as pertinent, and so these warning signs did not result in an immediate diagnosis. She persisted despite this scepticism and eventually got a consultation for Max with a testicular cancer specialist.

Our Royal Marsden consultant arranged the meeting and was present at the appointment. Having read about leukaemia, I remained composed because I thought Max's symptoms could not be a relapse of his cancer. In a sense, I was correct. Anxious, Sara waited for the consultation to start. The specialist scrutinised Max on an examination table for a few minutes and then asked our consultant to do likewise. As the specialist withdrew, he told me quietly that Max's cancer had returned. Meanwhile, Sara nervously joked with Max and our consultant before making a jovial comment to me. Unable to respond, I turned away and stared out of the window close to tears. After the examination, the consultants told us formally that my son had relapsed. Max was very chatty, full of spirit, and oblivious to the news. Devastated, we dared not show our feelings in case we scared him. Both of us were very frightened.

We regarded Max's second diagnosis as a death sentence because the consultants had told us during his leukaemia that the treatment was all or nothing. The first chemotherapy had been Last Chance Saloon, because any further strong medication left no second opportunities to treat this disease. Some say having a child diagnosed with cancer is comparable to grieving. Not true. Having done both, nothing comes close to real grief, but diagnosis or its suspicion is similar. We went through this scenario five times with Max, three of which resulted in a verdict of cancer, and each occasion was traumatic. How long did we have? How do you mourn the living? How do you crystallise, savour, and preserve each moment; every laugh, joke, and comment? You cannot. You can keep diaries, take photographs, or film videos, but these are shallow shadows of what you crave.

The profound injustice of the recent diagnosis struck us deeply, and it is only human to look for a reason and pattern in your lives. Having endured Max's first cancer, why did he now have a second? Why was this happening to our caring, sensitive, and loving child? What had we done to deserve this? We did our best as parents, so why were we being penalised this way? No one supplied answers to these natural questions, because there are none.

The news Max had relapsed was shocking enough, but the following weeks were confusing. Over and over you pray your consultant has made a terrible mistake, and it is normal to paint these landscapes of longing. Deep down we acknowledged the truth because we had seen these doctors at work. What they did sometimes bordered on the impossible; they knew what they were doing, but we still entertained these vestiges of hope. We tried to prepare our expectations as we desperately awaited further information. The waiting was interminable.

Have you ever really waited? Not queuing, but real waiting. Have you expected exam results, a birth, or the outcome of a car accident? Those nail-biting moments; take those and multiply them. Take the hours and days, the frustration and torment, and amplify them many times to understand our emotions. Parents sometimes wait weeks for the diagnosis and eventual prospects of their child's illness. They know something is radically wrong, but considerable time can pass before the realisation of their worst fears.

We went to see our consultant a few days after the consultation with the testicular specialist.

"I'm afraid we have little news regarding the prognosis. We're unable to chart the next stage without a precise knowledge of Max's illness."

We had researched the existence of swellings in AML. Sara asked, "What is this lump? It looks like a carcinoma, but Max had leukaemia, which doesn't produce tumours. Is it a chloroma?"

Chloroma is a rare sign of Acute Myeloid Leukaemia, and results in tumorous masses of white cells. The consultant looked surprised we were aware of this symptom.

"It might be, but we're just not sure yet."

I remained confused. We knew they could not treat Max again for leukaemia, so why was the hospital not taking any action? From my point of view, they should have been providing him with a quality of life as an incurable child.

"Why aren't you doing anything? Why is there this concern about treatment? If Max is terminal, then why are you not providing palliative therapy?" (Pain relief with no intention of prolonging life).

"No, Allan, you misunderstand; we're aiming for a cure."

This confused me even more. What was he talking about?

"What do you mean, after Max's leukaemia you said you could never treat him again?"

"I'm so sorry, I should have mentioned that there have been improvements since then. We said he must not have the same chemotherapy because his body could not withstand another dose, but there have been advances through new additional cancer drugs."

The axe was miraculously lifted, and numb resignation soared into hope. The relief was unbelievable. We moved from certain loss to possible survival. Having your child's death sentence lifted is strange and elating, but this is all relative. A second leukaemia treatment would be difficult, presented many risks, but was a huge step forward from being terminal.

Max's swelling appeared to be changing shape daily, but the Royal Marsden still could not supply a prognosis or treatment. Waiting for the test results led to an endless cycle of pacing restlessness and nervous surreal boredom. We desperately wanted an update to allow some sort of tangible future and enable us to grasp the time ahead. Lacking any news, we drifted, lost without a sail in a sea of helplessness.

Ten days after Max's diagnosis, our consultant rang at eight o'clock in the evening. Despite our earlier conversations, he explained that they still could not provide treatment because the hospital did not know the nature of his cancer. This type of bombshell became commonplace. Complications. You try preparing yourself, but they appear without warning.

"Hello Allan, it's David."

"Hi David, thank God you've rung. We've desperately been waiting to hear from you."

"I'm sorry I've not got back to you sooner, but there have been setbacks."

Alarm bells started ringing in my head.

"What's the problem? Why aren't we starting treatment?"

"We've not started therapy because we can't identify Max's cancer."

"But he's got leukaemia, hasn't he?"

"I'm sorry, but we're unable to confirm if that's the case. The cells look like AML, but the tests proved negative for this and every other cancer we've investigated."

I remained silent for a while. How do you absorb this information? Surely Max had relapsed with Acute Myeloid Leukaemia? Why did they not know? Where was the doubt?

"Are you telling me he has a different cancer, or another one as well as leukaemia?"

"I'm so sorry Allan, but we can't tell at present. I suspect you and Sara haven't been sleeping properly, and I can assure you I won't rest until we've found out what's wrong with Max."

The wavering of his voice in the last sentence confirmed his sincerity.

We received the formal diagnosis a few weeks later from a different consultant for reasons that soon became apparent. We learned that we were not dealing with our familiar disease, Acute Myeloid Leukaemia, but with another having the daunting name of Rhabdomyosarcoma (RMS), more commonly known as Rhabdo. This tumour has two subtypes, and one had a far better prognosis compared to the other. The hospital was unable at this stage to determine the specific subtype. Déjà vu. This latest devastating update was contradictory, because Max was playing and joking with his peers in the waiting room and behaving like any other normal seven-year-old boy.

The following week we received the news that the cancer had spread to Max's spine and his vertebrae were crumbling. He became immobilised and had extreme difficulty walking. This new disability was devastating, but not our prime concern. Our apprehensions related to whether the cancer had spread to his brain. Treatment is difficult once it has moved to this part of the body, because the blood-brain barrier blocks most chemotherapies.

Later that week our new consultant gave us the prognosis, and this news enabled us to better understand our circumstances.

"We know you're concerned, as are we, regarding the nature and timing of Max's treatment. I mentioned when we last met that there were two types of Rhabdo, and we've performed the subtyping tests. I'm deeply sorry to tell you, Max has the more aggressive form of the disease."

Yet again another body blow and wild loop on the roller coaster. Over a period of a few days, we had progressed from terminal to treatable, rapidly followed by the setback of a new cancer. Although this possibly survivable, secondary growths had migrated to Max's spine and now the consultant had told us the subtype of his latest disease had a poor outcome. Sara and I struggled to absorb the implications, but they did not sink in.

Rarely during these consultations did either of us show any emotion at this kind of news. You are not being strong or lack understanding, but the information is overwhelming and too hard to accept. My queries came thick and fast but on reflection were not helpful, because at times such as this you cannot reason clearly. I tried thinking as logically as possible, to work out what we needed to know, but missed vital questions or misinterpreted answers.

The consultant continued to tell us how she intended to treat Max's Rhabdo tumour.

"The drugs Max received during his leukaemia were extremely powerful and we can't use them again, because they cause damage to a young growing body while eliminating the disease. One could view it as fortunate Max has a different cancer, because we can try alternatives to destroy the tumour. There really is no second chance after the next set of therapy, because this time we're going for broke and won't be able to use any successive new drugs. We said this regarding his AML medication, but we'll be giving him a wide range of exceptionally heavy-duty chemotherapy for his tumour. If he relapses, then we'll have exhausted all practical options. Max's treatment will be particularly aggressive and again carries the risk he may die from it and not the disease. We have no other choice. As you know, if we don't provide treatment then he'll die."

We were very aware and understood these drawbacks. The consultant continued telling us more concerning Max's forthcoming therapy.

"This form of Rhabdo is aggressive and difficult to cure. It has the profile of reacting to chemotherapy, but rapid relapses are common. Would you be prepared to consider a discussion about experimental treatment?"

"How rapid are the relapses?"

"This subtype often reappears six months after chemotherapy. If Max survives for four years, then that's a reasonable sign of cure. I must stress that a third and different cancer is not out of the question."

Another little bombshell exploded. No cast-iron guarantee exists for any cancer, but this declaration suggested Max's long-term survival was unlikely. We took in the statement concerning a potential third cancer but forgot it for the following two reasons. The first was our immediate problem of coming to terms with his new cancer. Nothing else mattered.

The second was the enormity of the announcement, because its implications were too difficult to fathom. You undergo a narrowing of the mind's eye and your entire world compresses into the here and now. What happened a few days ago, whether good or bad, is rapidly lost. Today and tomorrow are all that matter because your worldview collapses like a concertina, and next week is irrelevant because everything telescopes and becomes focused into the present moment. They are other days, anything can happen, and there is no point in considering them. Their time will come, and when it does, you cope the best you can.

"What's the nature of the new treatment, and how does it differ from those you use at present?"

"As you know from before, the premise of therapy is risk killing the recipient, wiping out the disease, then rescuing the patient. With Rhabdo, we think the chemotherapy does not destroy all the cancer cells, and those remaining result in a relapse. We want to try a regimen involving far higher doses, now possible because of the improvement in recovery medication. If we'd given these increased doses in the past, then the immune system became even more damaged, took longer to recover, and the child died from minor secondary infections. We have a new drug called Granulocyte colony-stimulating factor (GCSF) which stimulates regeneration of the stem cells and immune system before infections have time to take hold."

"How many children have had this treatment? How effective is it?"

"It's being tried in a few hospitals, which have treated half a dozen patients to date. We can't judge the effectiveness yet because none have reached their six-month checkpoint."

Lots of parents face the dilemma of experimental treatment. Consultants ask the impossible; for you to pass a judgement on your child's life. What experience do you have? One can ask as many questions required during the consultation, or afterwards if needed, but what do you really know? A consultant once told me he would prefer to take parents out of this loop, because he thought it unfair to expect them to make such decisions. His statement horrified me, but I later understood this perspective because of the grim position faced by parents. It is not ethical to give an unproven treatment to a child without seeking parental consent, but conversely, they lack the ability to cope with this decision. No straightforward solution exists, and you require trust to resolve these dilemmas. How much faith do you have in the experts' judgement? They too are feeling their way through this precarious minefield.

Sara and I decided to put Max forward for the new experimental procedure. We were fortunate neither of us ever disagreed over the many choices regarding treatment. The potential for recrimination exists if a couple disagree and the child later dies. Whether a faulty choice caused the death is irrelevant. It is so easy for one parent to fall into the trap of believing the child might have survived had their partner made a different decision.

Transplant

Chapter 13

The doctors had scheduled Max for a bone marrow transplant as part of his tumour treatment. Chemotherapy has its risks and worries, but transplant moves these to another plane. It involves the annihilation of the remaining cancerous cells, but also destroys most of the existing bone marrow. This results in severe damage to the immune system and leaves the body defenceless to most illnesses.

Replenishment of the damaged marrow must originate from one of three potential sources: a sibling, an unrelated donor, or a previous extraction from the patient. Parents cannot contribute because at best they only have a 50% match with their child, not a close enough tally to prevent severe complications. Mismatch introduces the risk of Graft Versus Host Disease (GVHD). If the replacement marrow does not originate from the patient, then problems arise if the donated graft cells attack the host body. This causes extreme difficulties as the foreign cells assert their immune response. A child we had known for many months hung by a thread for a week as she battled GVHD. Her parents accredited her survival to the extraordinary dedication of the supervising Royal Marsden doctor.

Cell rejection was not an issue during Max's transplant because it involved the reintroduction of his formerly extracted bone marrow. Despite this, it was not a trivial procedure, and the chemotherapy had a 5% risk of being fatal. Antibiotics and difficult nursing support procedures supply the missing defences. This artificial protection is vital for the duration of the recovery period and is an intricate balancing act. Sara and I awaited with trepidation, were extremely frightened, and expected the effects to be worse than any of his former treatments. Transplant did not fall short of our expectations.

The procedure began with hyper-hydration, which involved flushing Max's body to prepare for the chemotherapy. He had a seven-litre intravenous drip over a twelve-hour period; a vast quantity of fluid for a child. Max and I were exhausted because he wet his bed ten times, and I spent most of the night comforting him and replacing his sheets.

A nurse injected the chemotherapy the next morning, which only took five minutes. This surprised me, because Max's earlier treatment had required multiple infusions spread over many weeks, but this drug was unstable and toxic, hence the single jab. After the injection, the nurse also administered medication to avoid complications that might occur as side effects.

After Max fell asleep, Sara and I waited anxiously. There were no immediate unforeseen medical issues, but we were horrified when he passed urine. The doctors had warned that it may include blood, but we had not prepared ourselves for the transparent crimson liquid that gushed forth. They reassured us once more that they expected this internal bleeding caused by the chemotherapy, and it continued for another four days.

The next day Max had the stem cell infusion that required the reinjection of his extracted marrow, which would help regenerate his immune system. A technician wheeled the replacement cells into the room in a steaming steel container, and Sara commented that it looked like a scene from a science fiction movie. The strange mist emanating from the vessel was boiling dry ice, which kept the cells at the right temperature before the procedure. Max became agitated as the nurse started the injection.

"Urghh, the taste of tomatoes is horrible."

"That's probably a side effect, but it won't last for long."

"Please can we take a break, so I can get used to it?"

"I'm sorry, Max, but we have to inject the cells into you as fast as possible."

"No, stop now because hot and cold waves are going from my head to my toes."

The nurse pressed on despite Max's protestation and he was violently sick. Having vomited once, he settled and there were no more incidents. He was pleased at enduring the procedure more successfully compared to his first stem cell infusion, during which the fear of the unknown had caused him deep consternation. He had received stem cells during his leukaemia treatment, but this was not strictly a transplant because it did not involve high dose chemotherapy.

Sara and I waited with trepidation for the symptoms the doctors had graphically described to us. Nothing happened. Perhaps we would get through this treatment unscathed? It seemed too good to be true.

I wheeled Max down the corridor later that evening, and we met his Chinese friend, Li Ming. She looked in the little wing mirror which he had attached to his wheelchair. "Maxie, Maxie, I love your mirror. Who is the most beautiful of them all?"

Without waiting for a reply, she squealed, "Me! But Maxie is the nicest person in the whole world."

I played with them both for two hours and had them giggling and in fits of laughter. We had to leave both Li Ming's ward and the corridor, because we were making too much noise and so continued joking and laughing in Max's isolation room.

Consultants assigned isolation rooms to patients undergoing marrow transplants or to immunosuppressed patients requiring controlled segregation from other illnesses. Fans pump purified filtered air into the rooms, keeping them under positive pressure to prevent the admission of bacteria if someone opens the door. Cleanliness is crucial, and visitors must wear masks and wash their hands with antiseptic solutions before entering. The doctors had not yet implemented these strict rules because it was the first day of Max's transplant. He was not at risk from infection, hence Li Ming's presence in his room.

Four days later, Max's symptoms confirmed our worst fears. He was exceptionally sick and had pain in his legs. When practising Kung Fu, my instructor told us to massage towards the toes in the case of a leg injury, because this enabled the Chi to flow and stemmed the throbbing. He had faith in this technique, which I had applied in the past. I kneaded his leg for an hour to comfort him. Grateful for my efforts, he gradually fell asleep.

As the chemotherapy symptoms took hold, Max stopped talking to anyone because sores on his mouth and tongue had created a sticky mess on his lips. He had seen the abscesses, which upset him, so I explained that we expected these symptoms. During this treatment, his faith in the doctors was almost as important as his trust in us. He knew we would question them, and if we were unhappy with their response would demand more information. If their assessment and the current state of treatment satisfied us, then this improved his ability to cope. The fact he could no longer talk made life exceedingly difficult. Our time together turned into a sad and sick game of charades, in which he grunted and gesticulated with his hands. Sara and I tried to interpret these actions, and mostly got by, but sometimes it was impossible to clarify his needs.

Max became extremely depressed, and his inability to express his feelings made matters worse. Frustrated because I could not reach him, laughter was the sole tonic as I larked around and played the fool. He responded with a twinge of a smile in the cracked and sore cavity masquerading as an excuse for a mouth. It worked. Sometimes the laughing hurt him, but his spirits soared. I found it uplifting reaching into my child's depression and hauling him back to some form of normality.

In the following days, the depression disappeared. It was not relieved, but Max passed into depths where this emotion has no meaning. Within a week the chemotherapy started showing its true colours: white, black, brown, green, and red. This vile rainbow resulted from the abnormal excretion of various bodily fluids. Max's mouth was white and ulcerating as the medication stripped his mucosal membranes. This symptom also hinted at how his intestinal tract was reacting to the drug. He had been vomiting for a few days, but now the spasms caused internal bleeding which led to the presence of blood, green bile, and coffee grounds. The latter are deep brown stains from dried blood, which showed the extent of the damage. There was little to retch because he could not eat or drink and was permanently on intravenous food supplements. His stools had become a black mess of dried blood and mucus and remained that way for over two weeks. Max's transplant had unveiled its full gamut of symptoms. The consultants brief you, but you are never fully prepared.

My scrap of a child contorted into the foetal position while retching and clutching his stomach to stem the pain from the convulsions. I helplessly watched my gagging wretch of a son as the tears rolled down his cheeks. Sara and I desperately wanted to help him, but he had passed beyond the grasp of our understanding. As he suffered these pitiful spasms, he would not let us cuddle him, hold his hand, or offer words of sympathy. This was his own private hell, where even the closest could not provide empathy or comprehension.

When Max wanted no intervention, Sara and I waited patiently and silently for a signal the heaving was over before we cleaned him. Afterwards, he let me stroke his legs or head. This carried on for ten days, with him retching once or twice every hour. Nursing him was exhausting, but I have no conception of how he endured this torment. On occasions he coped magnificently, but mostly he just suffered. Max was a ghostly and bloated wraith; an awful shadow of his former self. We struggled to provide relief, but he was in another world; one that we could sometimes break into and steal a smile. For us this made the difference between a good or bad day, but we wanted to help our poor son through his torture. We had seen horrendous treatment with Max and others but had never witnessed a transplant. Other parents had described the procedure and symptoms, but these accounts never conveyed their true reality. The first-hand suffering of the one you love more than anyone else on this earth is a different matter. Our pain soared above everything we had ever experienced as parents. We also became distant, lost, and numb. The barrage was too much, and so we correspondingly shut down, waited, and hoped.

Max reached a point where he just existed in a sea of suffering, but this slowly changed as he improved physically. As his body grew stronger, he returned to us with enough energy to show emotions, but then depression sank in and he told us how much he hated his life.

Sara and I jointly attended to Max during the day, but took turns going back to our house for the respite of an undisturbed night. The daily nursing left her run down and unable to sleep at home because of the stress, so I sometimes spent two consecutive nights with him. One day he became dismayed as I was preparing to leave, so I thoughtlessly offered him the choice of selecting who stayed. "I don't really mind, but I'd prefer it to be you." This reply distressed Sara, which left me perplexed. If we worked alternate nights, then she was too tired to cope, but if I stayed longer, she felt excluded. I was damned either way; a rock and a hard place.

Max's blood counts started rising two weeks after he received chemotherapy, so the doctors gave him GCSF. This growth factor kick started the regeneration of the bone marrow and his white blood cell counts trebled. The Senior Staff Nurse commented that he almost certainly had more neutrophils (a category of white blood cell) compared to the total of all the remaining children in the Unit. Two days after receiving GCSF, Max asked if he could leave our isolation room. It felt like the end of a prison sentence as I wheeled him around the hospital before returning to his bed. Our foray surprised the nurses, who did not expect to see him in the corridors so soon after his transplant.

The following day Max asked for a meal, leaving the Senior Staff Nurse dumbfounded because this was progress in leaps and bounds. Despite vomiting after the first bite, the fact he had even considered eating was a tremendous step forward. The doctors withdrew the antibiotics, morphine, and anti-sickness medication, resulting in his blood count plummeting before it rose again within two days. Nevertheless, he sank into a deep depression once more and would not accept any contact or communication. I told him how much I loved him, but a nod was his sole reaction. The immediate removal of the drugs proved premature, and he soon resumed the regime.

The doctors were not sure why Max's frequent puking continued unabated, because the sickness should have eased. I tentatively suggested to the ward doctor that the anti-sickness drug was causing the vomiting and nausea. Conscious of how illogical this sounded, it was a difficult proposition considering his experience. He was reluctant to follow my proposal of withdrawing the medication, but I replied with the infallible argument that he had nothing to lose given Max's continued retching. He agreed to go out on a limb and suspend the dose that day, despite the absence of the senior doctor. This deviation from the expected treatment bothered him. However, I was spending up to thirty-six hours watching Max like a hawk, knew his quirks, and how he reacted when something was wrong.

The following day the senior doctor walked into our isolation room during the ward round. Max was sitting up in bed chatting and playing, and the specialist commented "He's much better today, I think we'll keep him off the anti-sickness." The ward doctor caught my eye, smiled and winked, but he never disclosed my part in his decision.

Max's nausea disappeared, but he continued vomiting, though only once or twice a day. The doctors asked me to try persuading him to take oral medication because he could not stay on intravenous drugs indefinitely. Daunted because of his mouth sores, he looked at the pill in his hand.

"I can do it; I will do it. I'll take the tablet."

Max swallowed it and to our relief did not throw up, which was major progress. He was fully aware of my part in preventing his vomiting.

"Dad, why didn't they realise the anti-sickness medicine was making me ill?"

I explained that the doctors did not always have the answers, and that my suggestion resulted from spending lengthy periods with him; something not possible for them.

"Well, they should know. Daddy, you are the most lovely, nice, funny Daddy in the whole world. You're so," he searched for the expression, "dependable, but I'm not sure if that's the right word. You try so hard to get me better, and even if I dislike it, you still keep trying."

I was pleased to have done something concrete towards Max's recovery, and this built on the special bond between us. The increasing intensity of our trust was at the expense of my relationship with Sara. Often through the preceding week, Max appeared poorly when nursed by her, but fine when I spent time with him. Sara reported having an awful day and yet my sessions with him were relatively successful. I put this down to the fact the trivial things were getting to her, leaving her stressed and tired. I, however, slept at night and so found it easier coping. Max disproved this theory by announcing that he did not want Sara to stay because she "made him feel sick." This comment left her hurt and upset, and my instigation of the anti-sickness withdrawal did not help either.

Doing shifts is productive when parents work as a team, resulting in three or more hours in the overlap between nursing sessions. This time spent together enables both of you to discuss your child's condition, and how you are both managing and can help each other. The flip side occurs when it drops to half an hour or less, and you meet like ships in the night because of discord or extreme pressure. Sara bawled me out because the room was a mess and I had not made the bed, washed Max, or given him his medicines. One could justify this criticism if we had surfaced two hours beforehand, but not when we had woken twenty minutes earlier after a very sleepless night. Tiredness and stress are very destructive and sometimes drive you to the end of your tether. We were reaching the limits of our coping abilities, and I too was guilty of making similar accusations.

Two weeks later we received the results that initially determined the effectiveness of the transplant. Max did not need any surgery, his blood counts were high, and the number of tablets required were dropping. These perfunctory outcomes elated us, and we savoured them for as long as possible. Sara and I suspected Max's odds of survival had improved from less than 10% up to maybe 20%. This raised our hopes from total despair to light at the end of the tunnel. The elation lasted for two hours. Max announced that throughout the former week he had experienced aching in his left testicle next to the tumour site. This was worrying, and we reflected that even if his chances of surviving had increased, this still meant he had an 80% chance of dying. The consultants examined him straightaway, performed investigatory scans, and came to the consensus that another cancer was not causing his pain.

A later formal discussion with our consultant about the results brought our thoughts into stark perspective.

"The transplant was successful, and the tumour is receding."

"That's the first good news we've received for a while."

I was unsure how to phrase the next question, because it seemed presumptuous.

"Are you saying there's a possibility Max might get through this cancer?"

"These are early days, but it looks as if he's responding to treatment."

This was beyond my wildest dreams, and I fantasised the impossible, or at the very least became more positive regarding Max's future.

"Given the leukaemia may not reoccur because of how long he's been free of the disease, are we just looking at beating the tumour? I guess what

I'm saying is, if Max survives this treatment and doesn't relapse, then are we considering a cure?"

The consultant momentarily looked horrified, as explained by his next sentence.

"It's extremely rare for a child to get two disparate cancers, and in Max's case the evidence suggests a fundamental problem within his genes. He may fall into a group of what we call 'Cancer Prone' children. Even if he survives this tumour, there's a strong possibility he might suffer from another unrelated cancer."

Despite thinking this was the first time we had received this information, I afterwards realised that a consultant had informed us a few months earlier. Unfortunately, we had been too numb to understand or remember. The consultant was not being overly pessimistic but was protecting us from false expectations. This was not a cold ill thought out statement, but one made because he cared and did not want us living with false hopes. Unfortunately, his words fell on stony ground because we could only cope with the cancer of the moment.

The Royal Marsden gave Max a break for four days over the holiday period, after which we returned to the Unit for further therapy. A subsequent definitive scan showed that Max's tumour was shrinking significantly, and we returned home but attended the hospital regularly for consolidation treatment. The homecoming caused more problems than one would imagine. In a crisis you live for the immediate, but once that slips away you want everything to be as it was beforehand. I tried to take the long-term view, that of outsiders looking in on our sad spectacle of a story. Our prospects were incomprehensible, because objectivity made us realise the distance of our eventual goal. I sat and stared into space trying to make some sense of it all, but nothing had any meaning anymore.

Terminal

Chapter 14

wrote my concluding diary entries in mid-July 1996 after the completion of Max's tumour treatment. Life resumed an uneasy but welcome routine after my return to work, and this time Sara and I found it far easier shaking off the chains of therapy. Max was well, but we became concerned when he suffered from diarrhoea and earache. We called out a doctor, who immediately referred him to the Unit. The doctors diagnosed an ear infection and a possible perforated eardrum, neither of which worried us too much. We relaxed.

Everything changed in October when we raised the alarm. The siren sounded, the red button was pressed, and the bomb dropped.

The bomb exploded. Max relapsed.

Max was uncomfortable and had sporadic aches in his legs. Sara presumed the worst and so we returned to the Children's Unit. Our tumour consultant listened to our concerns and took them very seriously. Max's physical examination was not conclusive, so she booked immediate X-ray and ultrasound scans. We thanked her because these procedures always have a long waiting list. She proposed a Magnetic Resonance Imaging (MRI) scan, but the date conflicted with a planned break for Sara and the children in Wales. The consultant decided the trip took precedence, because a scan would make no difference if Max had relapsed. Prior to taking him to the appointment, he became upset when I told him we might need to shorten or cancel the holiday if he had to return to the Unit. I appreciated the prioritisation of the break but felt apprehensive, because any complications during the holiday leading to admission to a local hospital might create difficulties in returning to the Royal Marsden.

I did not go on holiday, because I had recently returned to work and felt guilty asking for more leave. Max's face cracked with emotion as the train drew out of the station, and he started to cry. I too fought back tears, fearful that I might not be there for him if he died. Sara rang me twice a day. His symptoms worsened throughout the week as the discomfort spread throughout his left leg and into his right groin. Regardless of this, he was enjoying himself.

Despite accepting Max's potential relapse, I slipped into a strange beguiling netherworld while remaining full of good humour and appearing to cope. Although these latest events did not affect me, I knew it was a sham because my self-protective shell was driving all fears and feelings deep into my subconscious. I sat at home, turning his symptoms over and over in my mind while scavenging for a rational explanation. Had the chemotherapy caused arthritis? Was an immunity problem causing these generalised symptoms? As time passed, my rationale became flimsy and more transparent. Max's throbbing increased, and Sara administered breakthrough painkillers when it appeared. I was grasping at straws while drowning.

Sara phoned me at work and said Max's pain was worsening, despite a telephone referral by the Royal Marsden to obtain stronger morphine from a local chemist. Two days later Max's leg started swelling. During another phone call, the Unit doctor suggested that the symptom may be a blood clot as opposed to a relapse. We decided Sara and the kids needed to return home, because we wanted Max treated by doctors who understood the history of his disease.

At five o'clock that evening I began my drive to Wales to bring the family back home. Just before I left, Sara told me she had found a lump in Max's right leg. He was in brilliant spirits, happy and mischievous, and these held my last hopes aloft because he sounded too well to have another tumour. We returned the following day, prior to my father-in-law mapping out the hospitals en route in case we got into difficulties. I still clung to the hope this was a terrible mistake; an unforeseen complication. Denial again.

We drove straight to the Royal Marsden, and during our consultation the Professor left us in no doubt the disease had returned with a vengeance. Sara and I struggled to gather our thoughts during this discussion, though managed to ask what options were available.

Minimal treatment with painkillers was the first of four possibilities that each required more intervention. Alternatively, they could give palliative chemotherapy, which might dampen the cancer and relieve pain but not achieve a cure. The third choice was similar but included palliative radiotherapy. The last possibility was unproven experimental treatment.

I queried whether a cure was a realistic proposition with trial therapy. The Professor replied that there had been long-term survivors, but cure required further strong chemotherapy and radiation, neither of which were practical options. After asking how long Max had to live, we were told that he might survive for three months if we were lucky. I doubted this statement because the tumour appeared to be growing at a phenomenal speed. The vicious early growth of this cancer had receded under the onslaught of intensive medication, but now it had returned.

During the consultation I chose the medication and pain relief option but remained silent. Sara had made the same choice. We discussed the alternatives after returning home and were glad we came to the same conclusion. We informed the hospital of our decision two days afterwards. Max's eventual treatment included radiotherapy, because it offered a better quality of daily life as his symptoms progressed.

A terminal diagnosis can lead to parents resorting to Doctor Shopping. This occurs when they refuse to reconcile themselves with impending death and seek treatment at any cost. After Max's leukaemia, Sara and I decided not to follow this path if he ever became terminally ill. Easy to say, but difficult to understand and do, and it takes immense strength and a mutual trust between parents and their consultants. It requires faith that you have had first class care and do not question the reliability of the final prognosis. The strength comes from accepting the terrible fact your child will die. In the cold light of day, letting nature take its course often best serves the interests of everyone concerned.

Parents often claim they are Doctor Shopping on behalf of their child. But has the ultimate parental quest for survival disregarded the patient's needs? The risks of most treatments and procedures are quantifiable, but terminal cases need further consideration. Quality of life is crucial while balancing the minimal chance of survival with the pain and suffering endured during that long haul.

Another problem occurs when taking a child abroad for novel experimental therapies as a result of Doctor Shopping. Structured and tested protocols exist in the UK to establish whether a treatment applies, and which subclasses of the cancer respond to it. The sole drive for this analysis is the wellbeing of the patient, but in some countries financial gain is a prime driver for medical services. In these instances, hospitals might try procedures without applying protocols, hoping to announce a miraculous new therapy. This, however, can lead to the following two scenarios.

Hospitals may offer the prospective treatment to children without performing prior reliable research, thus treating them as guinea pigs. In the second case, the doctors have done a study and correctly bias the initial choice of trial patients towards a responding subclass. However, if protocols are not in place, then the therapy might be wrongly proposed for children outside this category. This can occur because of the large potential financial rewards resulting from the flood of probable patients, despite the fact they should not be receiving the procedure. Neither example is ethical, because they do not consider the child's welfare or quality of life.

Parents searching for new and alternative treatments need to carefully appraise those not using a protocol. The media rarely discusses these issues, especially when many of the cures involve raising substantial amounts of money to fund their progress. People frequently support such causes based on emotions rather than facts.

Treating terminal children should never be survival at any cost. Time is not a good yardstick, quality of life is paramount, and a few months of worthwhile living far outweigh a year of further protracted intense medication and pain. These words may appear distant and lacking emotion.

They are not. The costs incurred by chemotherapy on your own and other children mean that extending treatment to the bitter end might not be practical or humane. Often you do no favours for the child or yourself, and accepting reality is much harder than continuing with therapy until death.

Sara and I lived under the shadow of childhood cancer for many years and watched the devastation caused by the disease and treatment alike. We were honest with ourselves, knew what we were facing, and had no illusions. There would be no futile last dash condemning Max to interminable therapy during his final days. Explanation of these issues is difficult, and after his leukaemia I remember trying to clarify these feelings with a colleague. Heated and angry, she said she would move heaven and earth to save her child. I agreed but replied that those little bodies have limits to how much pain and torture they can bear.

The news of our son's impending death produced an out-of-body detachment, and the consultation was unreal and distanced. The Professor asked us how we intended telling Max about his relapse and its consequences. Bewildered, we said we had not considered this vital task, despite bracing ourselves for its reality. Yet again we were unprepared.

A nurse fetched Max, and the Professor started his explanation. The intention was to spare us the pain of this awful conversation, but this turn of events was confusing. He told Max that the treatment had not killed every tumour cell, and this was "bad news" because the cancer had returned. Max was sitting on my knee and holding my hand, which he tensed and gripped tightly. He used this term when talking about the possibility of dying. Sara and I assumed he understood the discussion, but we discovered afterwards that he had switched off after hearing about his relapse. He did not absorb any of the later conversation, because the prospect of further treatment was too much for him to bear.

This prognosis induced a numb emptiness and calm, not the suspicious peace I had experienced while awaiting his diagnosis, but the genuine serenity of the sentenced. The waiting was over, and we had crossed the Rubicon to Class Four; the death of your child. Max later told me how unfair it was that he should have the illness again, and his comment summed up my muted anger. It was so monstrously horrendous that this intelligent and happy boy was now terminally ill with his third cancer. Tending to an incurable child was hard and stressful, and messed with my mind, body, and soul, but it was still not the experience I expected.

Lots of people commented on how brave we were after Max's terminal diagnosis. To me courage is a conscious and active choice, but this was not applicable to us because our reactions were a subliminal and primitive survival reflex. Events became so severe that they surpassed our earlier experiences, and so we created our own frames of reference because others had become meaningless. We passed beyond the moment to moment existence characterising our worst times and instead lived by our own private routine. Our lives were incomprehensible to an external observer, and we slipped into an alter reality in which we tried living normally with a dying child. We never felt strong, but just learned to accept.

The night after Max's terminal prognosis, I had a strange nightmare in which I was a serial killer in China. An unknown Chinaman colluded with me during the only murder in the dream, and later the police chased us through small alleys. After my capture, I received a fifty-four-year sentence at the trial. None of this made any sense to me, but Sara interpreted the Chinese connection as Max, and the prison term as my life sentence resulting from his loss.

How do you contemplate your child's death? I spent years considering this possibility and how people survive a bereavement. Many do not. I read about a father whose daughter died in a heart operation during her leukaemia treatment. He repeatedly heard her calling, "Where are you Daddy?" It became too much to bear, and he eventually committed suicide. I found it difficult reconciling myself with such stories. How do you come to terms with the subsequent pain? I did not, because these were fleeting thoughts and my sentient timeframe only extended to the present moment.

Sara and I tried discussing Max's terminal diagnosis with him and broached the subject after the consultation, but he was loath to discuss his new cancer. The following day Max and I watched "Friends" and "Caroline in the City." The humour in these television comedies amused him, and we often cuddled while watching them together. He laughed throughout the programmes, and afterwards Sara and I sat with him to have the hardest conversation imaginable.

"Max, what did you understand after seeing the doctors yesterday?"

"Well, my cancer has come back, so I suppose that means I'll need another Hickman Line and more chemotherapy." His voice was weary and resigned.

"That's not what he said. Didn't you hear the Prof. say that they'll be giving you Chemo, but not through a line because it won't cure you? The Marsden can't treat you anymore."

Max's forehead furrowed, and his voice cracked as he became very agitated.

"What do you mean?"

Sara burst into tears. "It means you'll die."

The scene then descended into a tragic black farce. I had lit a fire, but the chimney blew back and filled the room with smoke. Chaos ensued as I tried to stop the logs smoking as Sara cried and Max wailed. The fire alarm triggered, and I could not find a chair to reach up and deactivate it. Eventually I switched it off and cleared the smoke by opening doors and windows. We all calmed.

Sara and I faced a barrage of questions from our grief-stricken child.

"I'll never reach ten. There must be something they can do. Why can't they help me? It's not right I die so soon." Years previously, I had told Max that the doctors would only consider his leukaemia as cured after his tenth birthday.

"Maxie, they've done everything possible, and can't give you more Chemo because that'll kill you too."

"How will it happen? How will I die? When, tomorrow or next week? How long have you known?"

"We don't know how much time you have left Maxie and even the doctors can't answer that question. They'll give you Chemo tablets to reduce the disease, but we have no idea how or when you'll die. The Royal Marsden told us two days ago and said you might live for a few months. Do you remember last night when we tried discussing the illness, but you didn't want to talk? We intended telling you then, and we'd never keep secrets from you."

Max nodded, satisfied that we had not deceived him.

"I won't be able to go shopping for things."

"What do you want to buy?"

"I don't know, but I enjoy shopping with you and Dad. I'll miss you both, and my friends and Paula."

"We'll miss you too, but you can watch from heaven and will always be with us."

"I've been through so much. All that Chemo. So, so much. Why must I die after that? It's not right children should die so young; it's just not fair."

Sara and I sat with Max for another couple of hours, trying to answer his questions and offer comfort. I wrote these events in my diary two days afterwards, but my mind had already started shutting out this nightmare discussion. No one deserves such a horrendous conversation. After putting him to bed, we both cried and cried.

People questioned whether such honesty with Max throughout his illnesses was the right thing to do. In hindsight, I would take the same path. Apart from families within the Unit, no one had any conception of living with a cancer-stricken child. There are three options: conceal the truth, tell everything, or the middle road involving a mix of the two. We tried the first and last alternatives to no avail during the initial days of his leukaemia. However, you reach a point where both the parents and child need certainty. Any deceit becomes an unbearable burden because everyone realises the unspoken deception.

Your child at the end of the illness is no longer a child. Watching children mature beyond their years is painful, but you have no other choice. It is incredible, because they have a wisdom and courage that you may never achieve. This is not a father's rose-tinted view but occurs often, and leaves those in contact with the child feeling very humble.

The next day Max said that nobody should die before they became old, and that the doctors should prevent childhood deaths. Three days later I asked him how he felt. Full of beans and laughing, he replied, "I'm still sad, Daddy."

The following week, Max and I visited a cinema with two of his friends, but life smacked us in the teeth once more. When we reached the counter, the cashier told me no more seats were available, so we rented three videos to watch at home. One was "The Little Princess", and during the story the protagonist feels the shape of her father's face to remember him should he die during the war. That evening Max repeated these actions with me.

"I don't want to forget you, Daddy. If I become a ghost, then I'll come back and talk to you, but I'd miss our hugs. Please don't move to a different house, because I won't know where to find you."

Max's symptoms progressed as the days passed, but he was happy and not suffering too much throbbing. The swelling increased, and he experienced pains in his arm. The tumour growth had led to a clot that restricted the blood flow in his right leg, as suspected by the Royal Marsden. Max was prescribed Warfarin to dissolve the coagulation, a difficult treatment because of the delicately balanced juggling to find the correct levels of medication. We visited the hospital regularly for check-ups and to fine tune the doses. He later lapsed into incontinence, and this slow degradation gave me the impression secondary cancers were spreading throughout his body.

Max's understanding of his terminal diagnosis became more obvious as time passed, and we discussed what should happen to his possessions after he died. Max wanted Paula to have several of his toys, so Sara and I explained that people made a Will before their death. Later he came downstairs with lots of scraps of paper with "Will" written at the top, and below were a name and the items he was bequeathing. These actions humbled me because he continued with life, sorting out his affairs and laying outstanding business to rest. I went upstairs and cried after seeing one so young shouldering such a huge burden.

Other than his Will, Max was unwilling to discuss his death. This worried us and we wanted to put his mind at ease rather than him spending his last days in torment. Sara had a lengthy discussion with him about heaven and dying, which helped.

One day, while still able to walk, Max hobbled into the bathroom while I was having a bath.

"Daddy, I want to ask you a question?"

"Okay."

"When exactly will I die?"

I was pleased that at last the demon had revealed itself.

"Maxie, neither we nor anybody else knows, but the books I've read say you'll know when it's going to happen. I realise this doesn't help, and Mummy and I also desperately want the answer to your question."

My voice began cracking during the last sentence. Max looked at me, watching carefully, trying to see if I was telling the truth.

"Okay, I just thought you might know," and he tottered back to his bedroom satisfied.

Later, he wanted to understand the nature of his death. The hospital told us the most likely options; infection caused by immunity break down, or failure of his kidney, liver, or abdomen. The cancer also might spread to his brain, and we passed this information on to him.

Max needed faith to cope with his diagnosis, so I handed over a steel bullet I had used as a childhood lucky charm. Sara likewise gave him a set of children's transfer tattoos. He put a Chinese Dragon on his forehead, believing this would help him fight his disease, and two more over his kidneys for good measure. He looked strange and thug-like with his skinhead haircut and stark tattoos. We tried the ultimate talisman of love, but even this failed.

At Max's age you have many aspirations, fears, and insecurities. I tried to imagine his hopes and dreams. How does an eight-year-old contemplate the loss of family, friends, and everything important in his life? Can a youngster foresee death in the same way as we adults? I broached the question.

"Maxie, I worry because you never talk about how you feel. Mum and I want to help you, but we can't if we don't know what you're thinking. Are you scared of death?"

"No, not really. It's not dying that worries me, because I'll just die and go to heaven. But mostly I want to stay with you and Mummy and not be lonely."

Sara and I were prepared to try anything to help Max and so took him to a faith healer. How do I explain this? Humanity's scientific knowledge has progressed beyond belief during the last fifty years, but we still know little. In Victorian times a few arrogant people proposed that humanity had discovered most knowledge, but if true then advances should be painfully slow. They are not. Our understanding of the universe takes leaps and bounds, implying we are not at the conclusion of discovery. This, together with the fact the Chinese and Indian civilisations have used healing for many centuries, suggested we may gain something from seeing a healer. We needed hope and had nothing to lose.

Max was not keen on taking the trip, but I persuaded him that the visit might be helpful. We went to a suburban house and sat waiting in the hall. The middle-aged woman asked if I was working, and I replied that I had been nursing him for the last three months. She decided not to charge us, which I appreciated, not because of the cost, but because it suggested her intentions were honourable.

"Hello Max, how are you feeling today?"

"Oh, okay," he replied noncommittedly, being wary of strangers.

"I think you enjoy drawing and are good at Maths."

Max was astonished and told her this was true. It surprised me too, because neither Sara nor I gave her these details. On seeing my reaction, the healer said quietly, "Don't be shocked, sometimes we just know these things."

The healer chatted with Max, discussing his drawings before we followed her into the treatment room. He lay on a bed and she performed a "laying on of hands", which did not involve her touching him. After another couple of visits, he became too unwell to make the trips. I tried reconciling this healing with my concepts of the world and moulding a workable reality into what I had witnessed. It did not produce any answers.

Max's terminal days affected us in other ways. Paula's reaction worried us, and we tried explaining that his illness had returned, but she either did not understand or could not face the unwelcome news. We suspected the latter and approached hospital counsellors for help, but they could not tell us what she understood or how to soften the blow of his impending death.

After reading ten bereavement books, I worried how we as parents would cope after Max died. The consensus was that it took at least four years before the loss of a child ceased to overwhelm a parent. I found this a daunting prospect because we had already carried his cancer burden for three and a half years, which was pain enough. An often repeated message was that parents sometimes never recover from their child's death; not something I could contemplate. These narratives became disturbing and too much to absorb, because they suggested our journey had only just begun.

Leaving the house during the final stages of Max's illness left Sara and I deeply apprehensive, because we wanted to be beside him when he died. Having loved and cared for him for so long, the prospect of being absent during his last moments would be cruel. Most of the time friends performed our shopping, but occasionally we found we urgently needed something and had to make the trip ourselves. This likewise occurred with Max's medication, which the Support Team delivered to us, but sometimes we had to buy extra painkillers when the doses became ineffective.

Max did not slip away: he did not go gentle into that good night.

The End
Chapter 15

The doctors prescribed morphine for Max to counter his frequent pain. In the early days he asked why he needed the painkillers because if he relaxed quietly, meditating while staring into space, then he could exercise phenomenal control over his body. This changed as the aching worsened. The doctors instructed me to administer higher doses to overcome the discomfort, provided they remained within the constraints of the prescription. The first dose started at five milligrammes but doubled to ten after two weeks. Such a huge jump left me apprehensive, but again I had an awful lot to learn.

Sara and I waited with trepidation. Could Max survive until Christmas Day and if not, then how would we cope in future during the festive season? We were jubilant when Christmas Eve arrived. The October prognosis suggested he might stay alive from between three weeks to three months, and approaching the upper limit left us grateful. Not everything was against us.

Unsure whether Max still believed in Father Christmas, Sara and I suspected he had doubts because at his age other children often puncture such myths. He voiced his suspicions to me, but I denied that we supplied the presents. We had been so honest about everything else but wanted to preserve this childhood magic before his death. On Christmas Eve we waited for him to fall asleep, but each time we passed his bedroom he was still awake and excited by his prospective gifts. At eleven o'clock we were tired and ready to go to sleep. Sara crept in, caught him nodding off, and hurriedly deposited his presents before rushing out, hoping he had not spotted her.

Max woke at once, and pandemonium ensued as he shrieked and then called us. Sara had her nightclothes on and pretended she had come to his bedroom after hearing his calls. I could not appear clothed because he would know I had not gone to bed, so I stripped outside the door and draped a towel around myself.

"Mummy, Daddy, I stayed awake and the presents suddenly appeared like magic. I waited for Santa, but never even saw him. How does he do that?"

Excited, Max chattered nineteen to the dozen, and we let him open a few presents before calming him and going to bed. He would die with this little childhood belief preserved and keeping our son's innocence intact meant so much to us. Spending Christmas with him was the best present for me and Sara, left us exceedingly grateful, and was almost more than we could have asked. The whole family had a fantastic Christmas Day.

On January 1st, Max sank like a stone. He had a radiotherapy appointment with the Royal Marsden, but we did not think he could cope with the thirty-minute journey. Convinced he should no longer continue visits after this radical and sudden deterioration; I rang the hospital to explain our concerns. A terminal children's nurse came to our house later that evening and examined Max. She then sat with us to deliver her verdict.

"Max has taken a significant turn for the worse and I don't think more hospital appointments are appropriate. It's not fair on him and I suspect he's no longer capable of making repeated journeys to the Marsden. Our prime aim should be to limit his pain and provide the best quality of life possible under the circumstances."

"When do you think he'll die?"

After your child's terminal diagnosis, this question replaces queries about the chances of survival, but previously there had not been enough detailed evidence for a precise answer.

"You've been asking us that for a while, and I can't give you an exact estimate, though I don't think Max has much time left. I've said before that you'll know in your heart of hearts when he's going to die, which I suspect will occur within three days to three weeks' from now. If he survives for weeks, then I expect he'll be exceptionally ill."

Sara and I knew Max's time was nigh and showed no tears or surprise given her proclamation. We listened quietly and accepted this ultimate reality. The hammering home of this last nail meant we had to meet Death face to face.

"There are two options available. We can care for Max at the Unit, or he can stay here with you and our Support Team will supply daily help."

Sara and I had nursed Max through three cancers and continued doing so at home until he died. We suspected he would not have lasted long at the hospital and wanted the privacy of his death in the arms of his family. The Royal Marsden concurred, and neither I nor Sara regretted this decision.

My earlier morphine worries about the increase to ten milligrammes had become irrelevant, because his prescription had risen to hundreds per day. Max barely ate, and the tablets became difficult to administer and were yet another imposition on his shrivelled body. An alternative efficient method of administering painkillers is via a morphine pump, which delivers the drug through a thin intravenous line. Although it enables the patient to manipulate the dosage when the pain gets out of control, Max steadfastly refused this option because it required a tube into a vein. We tried persuading him, but to no avail, and did not pursue this treatment because our prime aim was to agree to his wishes. Instead the doctors offered experimental fentanyl opioid patches, which work like their nicotine counterparts to supply a slow and regulated release of the medication. The major benefit is their non-invasive application, and they were Max's preferred choice.

The pain continued, and we and the Support Team thought Max would die within the next few days. He had a sudden revival three days after the first downturn, when he recovered from semi-coma, asked to eat, and watched television. The doctors suspected this might be the last rally many people experience before dying, and he deteriorated again the following day as his suffering intensified.

Fentanyl is a powerful synthetic opioid one hundred times more potent than morphine, and the patches released their medication over a twelve-hour period. They were a godsend for drug administration, but Max's pain kept breaking through. Although I had received instructions on how to increase the dosage, I rang the Royal Marsden for further guidance. They recommended applying a further patch if the aching continued. The throbbing subsided, but I decided to apply another patch anyway, which was fortunate because the pain broke through a few hours later. It was so degrading seeing Max dissolving into an agony racked heap. Unhappy with the treatment, I tried to work out why it was not functioning effectively.

I graphed how often we applied the patches compared to the rate Max re-experienced pain, which suggested the upper limit of the prescription. It became obvious the aching was increasing far faster than the patches released the fentanyl, showing the inadequacy of the advised regimen. I took matters into my own hands and exceeded both the increase in dosage rate advised by the hospital, and the highest dose recommended by the manufacturers. Sometimes during your life, you must believe in yourself against all odds. This was one of those occasions.

Where is the morality here? I took the risk of overdosing my terminally ill son to prevent his excruciating pain, and my aim was to let him die with grace and dignity. Max had been through the mill, so why should this weak and emaciated child endure further misery? This raises the spectre of euthanasia, which provokes some forceful thoughts. I believe our laws are outdated and lack the care and ethics required in this difficult and sensitive matter. There are a few startling revelations if one takes an objective assessment and stands back from the emotive viewpoint. We relieve a horse with a broken leg from its misery to save it from pain. A vet respects animal rights and puts down a dog with an incurable disease to release it from its suffering. We do not perform these acts because of scant regard, but because we consider it as cruel to prolong any agony. Society takes a different view with human distress. We regard life as sacrosanct, and its termination is always a deliberate act of killing and classed as murder. This tenet of our legal system is worthwhile but requires further consideration in specific circumstances.

Violation of the principle of life raises real concerns for incurable patients. We should recognise and address this disquiet, instead of ignoring it, as was the case in 1997. There have been convictions for assisted suicide, but the moral stance of these verdicts is unclear despite the declaration of guilt in the eyes of the law. The legal system is inadequate when dealing with these issues and lacks euthanasia guidelines. Perhaps these are necessary? We have already approved the termination of a pregnancy to prevent an unwanted child. Not trivial, but incomparable to the brutal torment of many patients. I believe the terminally ill deserve the same respect.

The increase of Max's morphine dosage was no act of malice. I did not intend taking his life, but solely wanted to end his agony and suffering. I was prepared to accept the consequences of his death if I failed in my immediate aim of relieving his pain. Would I recommend this action to others in a comparable position? No, I would not endorse any of the major decisions we took, because each circumstance is unique. But I believe this was the correct choice in our case.

Afterwards, I went to bed for an unquiet sleep. The following morning, during breakfast, I asked Paula if Max was awake because I dared not investigate.

"Dad, he's not moving at all."

Cold and empty, I rushed upstairs and was relieved to find him still alive. The pain was under control and resulted in a second rally as he returned to us as a responsive child. We were thankful for this excellent day that vindicated my decision. He watched some television, chatted, and asked to go out.

"Dad, can we go to the cinema?"

"I don't think you're in a fit state to go anywhere Maxie, you can barely move. You can't even turn over on your own."

"I know, my mind wants to, but my body won't let me."

These are the words of a child gaunt from the ravages of his cancer, who the doctors soon expected to die. Max had shown an immense strength and gritty determination to carry on regardless throughout his illness and up to his death. He tried so hard and drew on all his reserves and resilience but suffered during his last days. Yet, despite the abuse by his cancer, it was cruelly ironic his mind was so strong and dragged his body through to the end. The Support Team could not believe how much he had improved. On one hand it was a wonderful sight to behold, but also challenging for us as a family. During the previous days he had become more and more comatose, and just lay on the bed moaning and writhing with discomfort. During those pain-racked times he became less conscious and was only partially aware of our presence. Sara and I had reconciled ourselves to the fact we had seen the last of our son as a cognisant human being. However, he had returned, a quiet smiling shadow, but still the Max we knew and loved.

The fentanyl dosages had flattened out and his intake was twelve hundred morphine equivalent milligrammes per day. This was two hundred and forty times the first dose, the increase of which had concerned me a fortnight earlier. The Royal Marsden doctors pointed out that my dosages were radical. I replied that Max was terminally ill, and I was not prepared to see him suffer. The risks of these high doses should be qualified. Opioids are excellent at numbing pain, but have several side effects, such as depression of the respiratory system. No "standard" prescription exists because correct usage requires the alleviation of pain present during administration. It is not fatal in this scenario because the body metabolises the drug. My dosages had caused concern because the patches were undergoing trials for children. The manufacturer set a prudent limit that I had breached, and my rapid increases were beyond the average child's tolerance level.

The fentanyl caused Max to hallucinate.

"Dad, why does that fly keep crossing the room?"

I had wondered what his eyes had been scanning, because every five minutes he tracked an object across his bedroom ceiling.

"I can't see any flies, Maxie. Tell me next time you catch sight of it."

We waited, and he pointed when he saw the insect.

"Look! Can't you see it?"

"No. Are you sure you're not hallucinating? Watch it carefully."

He concentrated.

"Oh yeah, it's not there."

He smiled softly.

"Why's that happening, Dad?"

I explained that the patches sometimes caused hallucinations, which he had also experienced during earlier fevers. Max found these harmless images amusing and grinned now and then, before slowly turning his head to tell me he was watching those funny flies again. After two good days, he began to deteriorate.

Sara and I nursed Max round the clock throughout his last days, and we were not only virtual prisoners in our own home but also within his small cramped bedroom. We had removed any extraneous furniture, and had three mattresses on the floor at night-time, but removed two when nursing him during the day.

A week before Max died, he asked Sara to leave the room so he could have a private conversation with me.

"Daddy, do you remember when you said I'd know when I was going to die? I thought it would be in five days' time, but now think I'll die in my sleep tonight. Don't tell Mummy."

This statement tore me apart, and I went downstairs and burst into tears. I told Sara, despite Max's request. We stayed awake throughout the night, and the following morning were like zombies and remained that way for several days.

The tiredness ground us down and it is easy to lose your grip on reality within such stressful circumstances. I slipped into magical thinking, when your hopes and dreams have no connection with the actual world. Surreal mind games became my coping mechanism as I clung to anything offering salvation. I remember my shock when a mother at the Royal Marsden told me her son would be fine, because his horoscope predicted good tidings for his star sign. This absolute and desperate conviction in these prophesies dismayed me because we both knew he was terminally ill. He died two weeks later. As an observer at that time, I had not yet reached the point where I could understand this contradictory behaviour.

I had a surreal fantasy we could overcome the disease and daydreamed of survival scenarios. Even at the end you do not lose heart; tenacious hope against all the odds. Could his body invoke an immune reaction to the cancer? The fact I had previously helped resolve his pain gave me faith we could still reach out for the Holy Grail of a miracle cure. I charted Max's liquid intake and bought glucose drinks to sustain his energy. The bruise on his hand appeared to be getting smaller. Were his platelets improving? At this stage he was semi-conscious, but drank if asked, which improved his overall fluid balance. He took small sips throughout the day but was cognisant enough to refuse the glucose drink because of the taste.

Max continued deteriorating daily, and he became too weak to roll over. Sara and I gently helped him, but turning a pain-ridden body is difficult without inflicting more suffering. On one occasion, she climbed on to the bed to help turn him.

"Don't, that hurts!"

Suddenly he flared up; a surprising reaction given his condition. He struggled to sit and looked at her before gritting his teeth.

"No! Don't touch me, I just want Daddy," he said vehemently before slipping back and closing his eyes.

Sara started crying, and I tried reassuring her by saying Max had intended no offence. Conscious enough to realise something was amiss, he whispered, "What's wrong?"

"Mum is unhappy because you wouldn't let her help while we turned you."

"I'm sorry, Mummy," he replied pathetically.

All of us were distraught. Sara was upset because Max had rejected her, and I was troubled by his preference for me. Close to his death, our semi-comatose child realised he had offended his mother.

I turned Max and then tried comforting Sara, but she refused any consolation. She said I had monopolised him, driving a wedge between them both, which was why he would not accept her help. This accusation has no simple response. I did everything possible and spent more time with Max because she found it difficult coping with the disjointed sleep. I tended the medicines because the battles with him and the resultant stress were too much for her to bear. My entire existence had become geared towards Max's survival. The result was a family split down the middle; Sara with Paula, and me with Max. Would our eventual circumstances have been any different if I had taken an alternative path? I doubt it, and hindsight does not deliver any clear-cut answer. Nothing was coherent in our lives anymore. We had passed the rational many months or possibly even years earlier. Living with our terminal child was harrowing.

I saw several children during their last days, which was often a pitiful sight. They are the Auschwitz children; a bundle of skin and bone, arms and legs like twigs, and shadows of their former selves. This is the physical description, but the psychological deterioration of a terminal child is another matter, and far more disturbing. A quiet burnt out look in their eyes reflects the true essence of their soul ebbing away.

I watched a documentary about Great Ormond Street Children's Hospital, which included a segment on six-year-old Sofia, who had Max's mannerisms and resembled him when he was bald. Her lung tumour had not responded to chemotherapy, so the surgeons cut out the eight-inch growth, but it reappeared two months later. She too had that burnt out look. The presenter asked her if she knew what job she wanted when she grew up.

"I'd like to be a model, or maybe a shop lady. No, actually I'd prefer to be a mermaid."

Such innocence; she died six weeks later.

Max had a full-blown fit on January 14th, a fortnight after he began his downward spiral. The doctors had warned us this might happen if the disease reached his brain. I suspected this was the case, because besides the seven discernible tumour sites, he had lost his vision in one eye. Sara and I had dreaded the occurrence of a fit, and it frightened and distressed the three of us. Max cried out desperately without warning from his dehydrated mouth. Arms and legs flailing wildly, his head shook from side to side as his face contorted with a ticking grimace. Random triggers resulted in a spastic chaotic dance of his facial muscles. Aside from the physical reactions, we could see genuine horror in his functioning eye; a look of total fear. I cried as I applied rectal sedative, followed by rectal morphine after seeing his detached patch. This was the sole instance I wept in front of him, and my sobbing caused him more distress. We were not sure if he understood our words, but he reacted to the tone and emotion within our voices. He gradually calmed as we spoke soothingly and gently stroked his head and legs.

I worried that we would remember Max in terms of his last days, as opposed to our wild ebullient boy. Eventually it did not matter, because the decline was gradual. The child is yours and always the one you have known and loved. You do not take the outsider's perspective when living with this slow deterioration that accelerates towards the end. Max's appearance shocked many who had not seen him for a while, but for us he was our child. The outward appearances are superficial and not what you recall. Time does her job well and leaves you with the person and not the body. I am grateful for that.

Not long after Max's brain haemorrhage, I made him a vow which affected me for the following two years. This do-or-die promise had the potential to destroy me. Like selling your soul to the Devil, there could be no return. I knelt by Max, who lay comatose, but this was irrelevant because I only wanted him as a silent witness to my pledge.

"Maxie, my little one. I love you so much. I've tried everything in my power to make you well again but have failed. You told me the doctors should stop children dying, well I promise to make a difference." I left him and wept.

"Make a difference"; what does that mean? This is an almost impossible feat, and I realised this undertaking might consume the rest of my life. I intended building complex software capable of generating its own programs, and if successful then the proceeds would go towards childhood cancer. My spare time for two years was consumed by spending hundreds of hours working on this project. I also read a hundred and twenty books on genetics, evolution, and complexity theory. It became clear I could not achieve my aims while doing a full-time job. Ultimately the promise lost its absoluteness, and I realised my life must continue even if I did not reach my objective. I abandoned the endeavour and drafted this book as a more realistic goal.

Max had another brain haemorrhage two days before he died, which was the last we saw of him as a sentient being. Sara and I felt cheated by this bleed because we wanted him to know we were beside him as he slipped away. It is strange trying to envisage your child's final moments. We did not want him to die in his sleep because we needed to say comforting words, and we also did not want him dying in pain.

We did not get the peaceful death we craved because he suffered three hours of Cheyne-Stokes breathing. This was a ghastly choking and wheezing as his lungs and the rest of his organs started failing. We preferred to be alone with Max and did not want medical staff present when he died. However, the noise became too distressing and so we called out our local doctor. She and the district nurse showed an exceptional empathy, did not intrude on this private family moment, and we were incredibly grateful for their presence.

Max died at 11:03 p.m. on 22nd January 1997.

The Royal Marsden had given us unsurpassed care, and Sara and I did everything in our power to save Max. We all failed. Life is like that sometimes.

When Max passed away, I experienced a huge physical release of tension. It literally felt as if someone had lifted a sack of potatoes from my shoulders; a partial relief of the hidden load I had been carrying for so long. After the doctor and nurse left, we brought Paula into Max's room, and told her he was at peace and no longer suffering. She and Sara kissed Max and cried before leaving me alone with him. I did not cry but wailed a howl of unbearable pain from deep down in the soul. Two hours later, I carried him to the hearse. He was so light, so limp, and it seemed inconceivable that Max had shrunken to this lifeless body.

I did not want to be present at Max's funeral because my feelings about his death were intensely personal. I would grieve alone and not air my sorrow in public. Two factors changed my mind, the first being that Sara and Paula needed my support. The second reason, triggered by the bereavement books I had read, was the consistent message that this ritual is not a pointless custom but has an actual function. This is the last farewell, and the recognition of someone's death. These books discussed parents who had not attended their child's service but had suffered years later because of their failure to participate in this process of letting go.

Sara and a friend changed my mind by suggesting we view the funeral as a celebration of Max's life. I never wanted a morbid reminder of my grief, but their proposal offered a different and positive perspective. After attending, I realised I would have regretted missing it until the end of my days. My preference was a small funeral with just the immediate family, and everyone else could grieve afterwards in a memorial service without me. Sara, however, persuaded me that many others needed to air their grief. We were deeply indebted to them, could not repay their kindness, and depriving them of their mourning was immoral.

Having decided to attend, I had robust feelings about the ceremony. I did not want a vicar mentioning God or being thankful that Max was no longer suffering. In an earlier conversation with Max, he had shown his desperate will to survive despite his illness.

"Maxie, are you afraid of dying?"

"No."

"I'm glad and it'll be better you're free of pain and don't have to battle anymore."

"No, that's not true."

No minister attended Max's service.

Sara had talked to Max about heaven, but I did not partake in these conversations because of my lack of religious belief. She reminded him of the children he had known and died and said he would be with them after his death. He was fascinated by the idea of reincarnation and announced that he would come back as an echidna. This is an Australian marsupial similar to a hedgehog, and was chosen because it was a Sonic video game character.

Sara asked Max whether he wanted a cremation or burial.

"I'm not sure about being buried. What if you move, then you won't be able to see me anymore? I want to be with you, Daddy and Paula. What happens to the body?"

"It'll fade away."

"What's left afterwards? Will it just be the skeleton? Will the worms eat me?"

"No."

"What happens if I'm cremated?"

"We'll keep your ashes in a pot and take them with us wherever we go."

"Oh yes, that's sounds much better. Can I have a grave and ashes, is that possible?"

Sara said he could not have both but could have a cremation and memorial stone, and this was Max's preferred choice.

"If you want, I'll make you a pot for the ashes and you could design the pictures decorating it."

"That's a good idea. I could draw Sonic and Tails and lots of Chinese things, like the Yin and Yang symbol."

Max did the drawings and Sara threw and fired the Urn, which sits in her kitchen as he had wished. His mischievous humour surfaced when she discussed potential messages to embroider on his coffin cloth. He chose two, and they reflected his impish sense of absurdity. "To infinity and beyond" was the sound bite used by Buzz Lightyear in the Toy Story film. Max was unsure of his ultimate destination, but this apt catch phrase captured his fascination with infinity. The second message was "That's all Folks", the closing sign-off for the Looney Tunes cartoons. This tagline summed up his thoughts, and he loved the irony.

Two hearses arrived outside our terraced house, before taking Sara, Paula, and me to the funeral, together with Max's best friend and his mother. It felt unreal, as if I was an actor in a scene from a film. Were we going to our son's memorial service? Yes, but it had not sunk home, and we were quietly numb. Our hearse drew up at the crematorium, but a queue caused a delay before we got out of the car. Fifty metres away a crowd waited for the service to start, and we became an awkward centre of attention. James, Max's closest friend from the hospital, ran up to me.

"Allan, why did Max have to die? He was my best friend. Why aren't you crying, don't you care?"

I knew this little boy well and had spent many hours playing with him and Max. What could I say? If I had answered truthfully, then I would have fallen apart at the seams. Saying nothing, I cuddled the sobbing child.

A crowd of people assembled at the Chapel door and waited as Sara videoed Max's coffin. It was wreathed in flowers and covered with the magnificent sheet they had both designed. The service started with "In the Summertime" by Mungo Jerry, a song loved and selected by Max. This upbeat tune celebrated his life, as did the primary hymn, "All things bright and beautiful." His schoolteacher and others close to the family read eulogies before the memorial address given by a friend. Having also lost a child, the task was much more difficult than it might have otherwise been. The reading was heart-rending, and we were indebted for his kind contribution. Paula, immensely proud of herself, commented, "Dad, everyone else is crying except me." Her time was yet to come. The funeral ended with the song "Let It Be" by the Beatles, chosen by me to start laying the pain to rest.

Afterwards we retired to a pub with many mourners, and that evening eight people came back to the house and drank much alcohol amid lots of laughter. I needed this emotional outlet and not the morbid gathering and deathly reflection I had dreaded.

The funeral commemorated Max's life and was a salutation to a child who touched many with his quiet courage. Sara and I thought he would have been proud and happy of how we remembered him, which was particularly important to us. People remarked on how this moving and personal service captured the essence of Max, and we felt we had given him everything he deserved.

Flanders Fields
Chapter 16

landers Fields. The battle has ended. There is carnage in the air, and wisps of smoke, death, and wreckage. Nothing is recognisable anymore. The land has been torn asunder, and is strewn with twisted metal, bodies, and suffering. It is the Outland and bears no resemblance to the rolling landscapes of the past. A pervading unnatural silence lingers after the years of fighting. Birds do not sing, and the stillness is frightening.

The palpable relief from the survivors can almost be grasped, light and fleeting, like the dancing of a passing cloud. But many silver clouds have a leaden lining, and those remaining realise this is not the end but the beginning. It is a start of the resolution of the years past and those to come, and the acceptance and a laying to rest of those daily horrors. This is not an easy task and presents unexpected new challenges and confrontations.

Slowly the people rebuild their fractured lives and despoiled land. The bodies have been buried and the shell holes filled, but the survivors know these are merely superficial deeds. They watch as ghosts wander the rolling fields; they listen to the distant echoing cries of pain, and the respite of the laughter that used to punctuate and hold the terror at bay. The land can be cleared and tilled, but these wraiths and memories are more difficult to exorcise, because they live in the minds of those spared.

Bulldozers and spades, flowers and graves; these tools cannot expunge the pain. The poppies grow, and a carpet of red calm spreads across the battlefield. Nature and time take their course and cover those indelible scars.

Years pass; children and adults alike are killed and maimed by the unexploded shells wreaking their delayed vengeance. There are fractures and rifts that never heal, allegiances and treaties that were never kept; the politics of war are remembered long after the peace. There are resentments and unsettled scores. Together we stand and together we fall; it worked well during the war, but nothing matters much anymore.

The soldiers return home, hoping, yearning for the pastoral of yesteryear, but life has moved on. They shuffle from the alien to the alien. Everything has changed, and their dreams have turned to dust. The old world has been swept away, leaving them so weary; they thought the fight was over, and sometimes their will to carry on falters. For some nothing remains because they have given their all, and these lost souls wander adrift and listless.

The world looks on and grows bored. A fleeting while passes before another war, another battle. Everything is forgotten. Those afflicted by these inexplicable barren scars do not forget. In this displaced world the unreal became the normal, but now they faced the long haul back.

Max's death was my Flanders.

The next day, I dismantled Max's bed and shampooed the carpet. Sara cleaned his room, packed away his possessions, and distributed his toys as requested in his Wills.

Within the following weeks we realised our son's needs had permeated our lives for so long, and in ways we had never even appreciated. We missed his laughter and tears, his video game playing, and attending to his calls throughout the night. Our loss of Max irrevocably tinged other events, such as mealtimes and watching television together. We needed a new pattern; a different way of living.

It was strange not providing any more care. No more pills, sick bowls, cleaning his vomit or wet bed, or other aspects of our former existence. We no longer worried about the next symptom and temperature or had a total preoccupation with his cancer. With that came the realisation of how abnormal our lives had become, and the readjustment needed to return to reality. Many paid Sara and I tributes for our courage and efforts in helping Max fight his illness, but these words did not afford us any comfort. The bottom line of his death was the huge meaningless waste of a child who had shown such guts, character, and self-awareness.

I returned to work with a determination to resume my career. To function back in the real world, I relied on a façade I presented to everyone outside the immediate family. This survival mask suggested I was coping, but its true purpose was to stop me having a complete breakdown. Dropping this sham would cause the avalanche of pain I was desperately trying to stem. Minor snow flurries and the occasional collapse of a drift were my only way of expressing this landslide.

Soon after Max's death, my pain alternated with an absolute gut vacuum, a very conscious physical emptiness. Two months after he died, my sister asked how I was coping, and I replied that if this was grieving, then I might get by. But I did not trust these emotions, because troubled stirrings hinted at something far more serious lying on the horizon. These were prescient thoughts given later events.

I started sliding downhill two months later, when a suffocating lethargy overwhelmed me. It felt like living in treacle because my brain was working in slow motion, and I became completely apathetic even though I had things to do. Despite functioning while at work, at home I dismantled the walls built to stem the grief and curled up in a ball on the sofa. Occasionally the television was on, but it made no difference because I just stared blankly into space. Despite having experienced similar symptoms of depression soon after Max's first diagnosis, this time I had no more strength left and lost interest in everything. I was inexorably shutting down and starting to fall apart.

I thought I was managing, but the control slipped away as I sank into deep depressions every weekend. Sara recognised that I needed help and had a severe problem. Reluctant to accept support, I assumed this was just another mountain that required scaling, like all the other hurdles I had faced.

These bottomless black holes lasted longer and longer, and I only agreed to receive help after they overwhelmed me. A major taboo still exists with seeking mental health advice, and this is an irrational and culture driven fear. There is nothing to lose bar the recognition you have a problem. After seeking support, I accepted the solace provided.

Sara approached the bereavement charity Cruse and arranged four counselling sessions for me at home. The Counsellor probed with considerate questions to discover my feelings about Max, his illness, my life, and the depression. I thought I understood my emotions, but what spewed forth frightened me. On seeing the past years objectively, I realised I had never recognised the true intensity and complexity of my bond with him. I was his father but had also become his brother, best friend, nurse, and doctor. Sara and I had grown apart because I had given him all my love and affection. When he died, many of the traditional aspects of a parent-child relationship had reversed because I found Max's courage and fortitude incredible. A child normally looks towards the parent as their role model, but I now sought similar strength and faith to confront the unknowable with so much acceptance. This and more poured forth in the sessions, but it became conspicuous that besides losing my son, I had lost my will to survive. The counselling helped my voidal emptiness, but a few months later I started experiencing something far worse.

Flashbacks had always struck me as demented film loops, a nonstop rerun of some awful event. But mine were not vibrant hallucinations, there was nothing to see or hear, just an intense playback of stark emotions. These living dreams reared without warning and were so hard to face. This crushing and numbing reality left me shattered and quivering inside.

I cried after the flashbacks, which occurred most days early in the morning when driving to work or in the evenings after returning home. They often came in cascades, the first triggering the second without any link. Rarely focussing on my worst moments with Max, they were fragments of our times together; long forgotten snippets of events and conversations. Although many were innocuous in their content, they were terrifying because I experienced each episode in its entirety. The memories themselves were generally happy ones, but they intensified the loss and that I would never see Max again.

The pain resulted from this lost world replaying itself moment by moment in real-time. Sometimes they were not actual events, but imaginary situations conjured up in my mind's eye, and yet again these were not the flat fantasies of normal thought. The flashbacks acted as a huge magnifying glass, amplifying the vast numbing reality of my loss. The blinding intensity and pain of these sensations is so distant from everyday existence, and almost impossible to describe to anyone who has not experienced them. Out of everything I lived through during the cycle of Max's illnesses, death, and my bereavement, nothing compares to the pain I suffered from this total emotional immersion. They were relentless and occurred almost every day in one form or another for eighteen months before subsiding.

I experienced less frequent dreams and nightmares, which were just as unpredictable and almost as upsetting. In one dream I was sitting on the shoreline at my old home in West Wales, when I spotted a tiny figure in the distance running across the sand. Max had his arms flung wide, as he often did, ready for an enormous hug when we met. Awestruck, I wondered how this was possible for my dead son. He ran into my arms laughing, and I cuddled him, only to awake and discover this was yet another cruel illusion. As with the flashbacks, many of my dreams had no connection with his cancers but were vivid memories of him as a cheerful child. They were cherishing little scenarios of harmless talk and laughter, which celebrated his life and not the suffering associated with his disease or death.

My worst nightmare best encapsulates my feelings during that period. An unknown pursuer chased Max and me through woods late at night, and we sought refuge within a brick building. Cautious, I held Max's shaking hand as we stepped inside the cold, dank, fifteen-foot room. A dim light from a naked bulb hung from the ceiling. Relieved at having reached the safety of this sanctuary, I closed the door, but a shadow loomed out of the darkness.

A huge and terrifying seven-foot black raven approached with a silent and threatening menace. I placed myself between my son and this dark avenger to halt its slow and purposeful advance. It paced around us, staring intently at Max, who appeared to be its sole prey. Unable to move a muscle and petrified with fear, Max whispered, "Help me, Daddy." He remained transfixed and terrified, as I too circled and protected him from this fearsome bird. Realising he needed an escape route, I ran to the door, opened it, and screamed for him to get out. Paralysed with terror, he stood stock still. The raven lunged for the kill.

I awoke sweating and distraught.

Other unexpected events supplemented the flashbacks and plunged me into emotional turmoil. I turned on the television and saw films Max and I had seen together in the Unit. He loved movies including visual gags, such as "Naked Gun 2 ½", which we watched over and over again. He roared at the jokes and often rewound the video and forced me to watch a gag again, despite having seen it countless times before. So many giggles, so many memories, and so much pain.

A walk into town unleashed reminders of the countless visits with Max in his wheelchair. I found it tough watching boys his age, how they resembled him while fooling around, and realised that he would always be my eight-year-old son. What would he have looked like had he survived his cancers? Seeing his school friends was difficult too, because they moved on, got older, yet he remained frozen in a memory time warp.

When I restarted work, I used the road leading to the hospital, which triggered memories of the urgent trips Max and I had made together. Two of these occurred in heavy snowfalls, and we had passed several cars abandoned and scattered beside the highway. On both journeys he had a fever and infection, was immunosuppressed, and would not have survived long if we had become stranded. After he died, driving along this route brought flashbacks of those and other visits to the Marsden, so I changed my route to escape these constant painful reminders.

Other incidents occurred where I found myself unexpectedly cast headlong into the turmoil again, despite my belief it had diminished. I needed a briefcase and visited Sutton, the nearest town to the Royal Marsden. My quest was unsuccessful, so I wandered around the shopping centre before arriving at a table where we and Max had gone for a hamburger after his Rhabdo admission. He had sat pale but happy and wore his cardboard sick bowl as a hat. Sara and her sister were joking with him and I remember being quiet, watching him eat, and wondering how we could cope with his second cancer. As these thoughts swirled, I realised I was looking at a mum from the Children's Unit. I walked over but had trouble talking. Sympathetic, she told me how she often thought of us, and we spent ten minutes together. At one point she commented, "The bottom must have fallen out of your life", and these words summed up my feelings. Afterwards, I returned to my car and bawled my eyes out. These ghosts and memories often sprang up and caught me unawares.

Priory Park is a large scenic estate including green open space bordered by woodland, and Paula and I visited regularly because she loved walking or cycling round the lake. Recollections of an incident used to flood back with each visit. Whenever we reached the water, I remembered the last time going there together as a family. It was just before Christmas, a month before Max died, and we had taken semi-stale bread with us to feed the ducks. Taking great delight in eating half of it, he giggled when asked where it had gone. He was in a wheelchair, and I remember watching people scrutinising him. Despite looking thin in the face, nothing else suggested the seriousness of his condition. I wondered if they realised this child was terminal but suspected his laughing and joking dispelled any such thoughts. I endured these suffocating memories on Paula's behalf until repetition lessened the pain.

Other places became out of bounds because they too inundated me with earlier memories. We as a family had visited London Zoo a few times, but each episode and nuance had etched itself deeply. It took eighteen months before I was ready to visit again with Paula. I stopped going to Wales for holidays, because reminders made the visits too painful. We had gone back, only to discover a vast gaping hole that was Max. I returned to the Royal Marsden four times in the year after his death. On each occasion I ended up sitting in the car crying long and hard for a quarter of an hour. But despite this, part of the load had lightened. As time passed, I whittled away these prohibitions. Overcoming these triggers involved heartache, but I slowly learned to face these fears.

Bolts from the blue resulted in the past and present colliding without warning. After climbing on Paula's bunk bed to get something from the cupboards I had built above it, I discovered the word "Daddy" scrawled in pencil on the wooden border. I asked Paula about the scribble and was shaken by her reply that Max had written it several weeks before he died. It was bewildering, and as if he was reaching out and trying to talk to me. I wanted to ask "Why?", chat with him, cuddle, and make sure everything was well, but the lack of these comforts left me with just a void.

Looking at Max's photos was upsetting, and an unexpected sledgehammer blow if they were in someone else's house. His photos filled our home, and after Sara commented that she only looked at them when able to bear it, I realised I too was subconsciously avoiding them. We bought a video camera after his leukaemia and had sixteen hours of family recordings. A year after his death, Sara went away with Paula for a weekend, so I watched the videos. It was painful, and I was glad I did so, though never repeated the experience.

Memories are curious because sights and sounds can invoke a whole vista of experiences you never realised existed. This is particularly so with music, and the R.E.M. song "E-Bow the Letter" captures those moments in my life. I first remember noticing this track when Max and I were halfway to the hospital. When I asked whether he minded if I turned up the radio, the lack of reply reflected his withdrawn mood. I listened to the music, which became my song of the moment because the strange lyrics fascinated me. This and the song "Leave" became linked with so much pain and later I bought the associated album. I remember listening to these songs in our kitchen late at night. Sara and Paula had gone to bed, so I increased the volume and drank to dull the pain. The songs played, and I moaned and howled for my lost child. I talked to Max in those early days after his death, not because I thought he could hear me but because it helped soothe the pain. This continued for hours until I became drunk and cried out. The emotions from that and other similar nights flooded back whenever I heard E-Bow. Pure distillation, pure pain. Little by little, these and many other songs ceased to bookmark Max's death, and the sensations became subdued, distant, and receding.

A curious by-product of my grief was a strange amnesia. As time passed, my mind erased entire episodes from Max's illness. Sara mentioned one child from the Unit, but I drew a complete blank and lay awake much of the night trying to picture this child and her family. When my memory returned, I remembered that I had talked to this girl and her mother most days during their stay in the Unit. I also could not recall the location of the ward kitchen, and this forgetfulness extended to the names of nurses or doctors. Despite having lived there for so long, much had become obliterated.

I faced a further unexpected mental reaction to Max's death; a stark clarity and decision making which before would have left me unsure. This occurred in both my personal and work life, and I saw clear-cut resolutions while others dithered. I wondered whether this conviction was justifiable, but later saw a documentary on trauma which explained this odd phenomenon. It is caused by hormone changes during the fight and flight response, and which swamp indecisiveness.

Another well-known trauma reaction is the re-evaluation of your values and beliefs. During and after Max's leukaemia, I swore his disease would not dominate or change my life. Dominate it did; but it did not fundamentally change me. His death was another matter, and I do not believe any parent can say the loss of their child has not irrevocably altered their lives.

How does a family of four adjust to bereavement? Our nuclear family did not explode like a bomb, but slowly unravelled at the seams. Two grieving parents and a sad child; all immersed in pain.

I had a disturbing dream about Sara, in which I mulled over a photo of a woman in blue. Given that I had been so in love with this mystery woman, I could not understand why we had married. I awoke shocked and confused when I realised the picture in the dream was of Sara during her twenties. Our relationship had suffered strains prior to Max's illness. We sought help but put it on hold during his leukaemia, the years waiting for a relapse, and throughout the treatment for his subsequent tumour. After his death we found we were strangers living in the same house and our marriage ground to a halt. When we discussed separation, it was as if my earlier life had never existed and had no meaning. We had been married for thirteen years and been through a lot together, but I could not understand our shattered lives anymore.

One desperately needs the love of a spouse when your back is against the wall and the odds are stacked against you. This often works, and couples go through hell and high water together managing challenges. But not always, and sometimes neither of you is in any position to offer crucial mutual support. Our grief was an all-encompassing fire, smothering everything before it, and we staggered burnt out and coughing, wondering what would happen next.

After Max's death, all held at arm's length came to the fore as we started assessing the costs. What had happened to our lives? We no longer needed to forsake ourselves for him anymore and awoke from this nightmare desperately trying to cope with our grief. Neither of us believed any love remained in our marriage and we decided to separate. Despite our decision, it was not financially practical, but this changed when we parted a year later.

Leaving the family home was a frightening prospect; such a long time spent with security, though little stability. I moved out and rented a three-storey terraced house a mile away, enabling me to still visit Paula and support Sara. Not ready to live in a cramped flat or share a property with anybody else; this building had barely enough room for my ballooning grief. I crawled like a maimed animal trying to find somewhere to hide, to lick my wounds and recover. Isolation. I did not have enough strength anymore; I had no love left for anyone, not even myself. Attempting to recover from my injuries consumed all my energy, and I needed time and space to reconcile myself with everything that had befallen our family. Working obsessively on my promise to Max during my spare time, this needlepoint of concentration helped divert me from the heartache.

Little animosity existed between me and Sara, which caused confusion amongst friends, but they had no conception of the life we had been or were going through. Sara said, "That's their problem", and any explanations were meaningless. After we parted, I often looked after Paula while Sara went out for the night. The rooms, the photos, and other triggers invoked a barrage of flashbacks. Babysitting was unbearable, because most nights I cried my way through the evening, and my leaving the family home was a necessary step for recovery.

During this period, I had another unexpected reaction after Max's death and became involved in a complex relationship. Having felt nothing but void and pain, I now experienced soaring elations followed by deep depressions, which alternated without warning. The woman and I developed a close friendship but progressed no further. Afraid my emotions might be a side effect of my bereavement; I could not face more hurt for anyone. I needed reconciliation with Max's death before I could ever hope to live normally again.

After my departure from the family home, Paula's relationship with me initially bordered on antagonism. I wanted to heal the rift, but the loss of her brother and departure of her father had deeply hurt my little girl. Her life had been immensely difficult for one so young. Paula rarely joked and cuddled with me because she resented the love I had given Max, and her rejection hurt me deeply. I focussed on the time we had lost to his illnesses and we started to share new games, running jokes, and built a routine important to us. Our day together each week helped me forge a fresh outlook, and the relationship improved during the next two years as we built new bonds and grew closer.

On the first anniversary of Max's death I went to work, as opposed to turning it into a Memorial Day. I did not visit his plaque in the Children's Garden of the Crematorium, which we used as a focus of remembrance. Taking leave would have resulted in me spending the day crying and left me depressed for the rest of the week.

I attended a Christmas party a year after Max died, and I was conscious of the couples' present and uncomfortable being alone and single again. I coped well until speaking to a Welsh colleague I knew vaguely. We chatted about my original hometown of Cardiff and moving to London, but then talked about our families.

"Do you have any children?"

"Yes, I've a daughter aged six."

"Have you thought of having any more?"

Neither Sara nor I ever flinched from the truth when presented with unforeseen queries about our family.

"You don't know?"

"What do you mean?"

"I used to have a son, but he died a year ago from cancer."

Mortified, my co-worker apologised and did not know what to say, but I told him not to fret. Never denying the harsh reality of Max's death, this incident happened often in different contexts. I fell apart after that conversation, became drunk, and sat alone in the car park crying in the rain. Gradually I cut myself off from everyone around me and never attended an office party again.

A child's death is one of the most traumatic events a person can ever experience. Cruelly, and with twenty-twenty hindsight, it is nothing remotely like the aftermath. My grieving started with something far worse; pure agony, anguish, and suffering. The bereavement began as a quiet void that grew and grew. Nature abhors a vacuum, and so a cacophony of emotions created an ever-growing whirlwind of pain. This tornado of grief rapidly spun out of control, but diminished to hurricanes and gales, and it took two years before I could start rebuilding my life.

I felt nothing but hollow after Max's death; a sense of enormous loss, a huge vast endless desert of desolation. I wanted to comfort and talk to him, to have his little arms around me as we hugged, watch him sleeping, or doing anything else involving our times together.

The grief flooded my life and reduced me to nothing. Weekends were the most difficult, Saturdays less so because Paula came to stay and diverted my attention. Many Sundays began with crying when I arose in the morning, and which continued throughout the day. Sometimes I tried sleeping to escape the heartache, but this proved to be a temporary relief because the tears continued when I awoke. The intensity was brutal and far worse than that experienced during Max's illness. This was not childhood sobbing, but much more physical, an all-consuming twisting of your gut into a coil as a vice crushes your chest. This constriction resulted in an erupting explosion that left me reduced to rubble and extremely withdrawn.

As my wellbeing deteriorated, I became more aware of several contributing factors. I needed close friends with whom I could share my burden, but they lived far away. The extended family offered more than enough support, but I declined because of their proximity and immediate connection to Max's history. My two sisters understood these sentiments and occasionally rang and quietly tolerated the monosyllabic answers they received. However, my mother rang every week and tried holding a conversation where none was available. She needed to care for me but did not understand that I was in no position to accept her words of solace. I had immersed myself for so long in my family, my work, and renovating our home, only to discover I lacked the support mechanisms desperately required.

I no longer had anything in common with anyone anymore and did not chit chat because no one understood the only thing of importance in my life. My confidence and ability to relate to others waned as I retreated from the world and did not look people in the eye when talking. Unable to view anything without becoming intensely emotionally involved, other's hurt developed into my hurt and worsened the pain. I stopped watching films or reading papers, because mistreated children or suffering in wars reduced me to tears.

I donated my prized library of four hundred books to the League of Friends, who sold them second hand to raise money for the Royal Marsden. In lots of ways this was symbolic, and part of the cauterisation involving the dissolution of my past life. Our house had required extensive renovation because it had been used as a bedsit. Before Max's illness, I worked for five years over the weekends, because this was the only way to afford a home meeting our needs. I was proud of my efforts, but now nothing mattered anymore.

Many mothers and fathers retain their connections with other Unit parents because of the camaraderie and understanding not found elsewhere. However, I did not sustain these contacts because I needed to escape from that past. I could barely cope with life as it was, let alone how it had been. Sara updated me on the status of families we had known at the Marsden. It was heartening to hear a child was well and a family was coping, but the unwelcome news devastated me. I heard of the deaths of eight children and one parent during the year after Max's death.

On one occasion Sara phoned to tell me about the deaths of two children and a parent. I received another call from my cousin ten minutes afterwards but was unable to speak and just sobbed. This was the only occasion throughout my bereavement I exposed my grief to the outside world. Generally, the tears were mine, and mine alone.

Despite my desire to distance myself from childhood cancer, I later experienced a strange and cruel twist of fate that no longer surprises me. The unexpected jumped out from the black shadows so often, and after a while I became immune to these calamities. Roughly three months after returning to my job, the woman in the next desk told me about her niece's cancer diagnosis. Having come back to work to escape from Max's illnesses and death, this news horrified and upset me. I waited for more information, but after some confusion it turned out the girl's illness was a misdiagnosis. I felt deeply sorry that the family had to endure this pointless misery.

These same parents underwent the turmoil again six weeks later with their son Liam, and this time it did not involve a diagnostic error. I found his cancer deeply distressing, especially as a third hand observer. I had experienced many other families' problems in the Unit as an equal, and had frank discussions about the treatment, fears, and realistic prospects regarding their child's cancer. Being an outsider was different. Many of my colleague's comments suggested an ignorance of their implications, or that the hospital was only feeding the necessary information. I listened and sometimes cautiously framed my doubts or partially explained her remarks, but never felt able to speak my true mind. After a few months, she described a set of symptoms I knew were serious and suggested a low chance of survival. She was unaware of the consequences and I said nothing. I cried in my car before returning home. Afterwards I wrote a letter of condolence and support to the boy's parents, because I would be too distraught to do so when he died. Liam displayed the fortitude shown by Max and passed away three months later. I sent the letter to his mother and father, together with book lists and booklets providing practical help for surviving a child's death.

Fifteen months after Max died, I reached my nadir; the lowest point in my journey. My "Road to Damascus" occurred while driving along a small country lane, when another unexpected tremor struck in my quake ridden world. The thought "I just don't care, nothing matters anymore" came out of the blue and with no real precursor. A friend had expressed a similar reaction after his son committed suicide. In my case this led to a gentle but major frame shift; the subtle difference between recognising your world is collapsing and the realisation you no longer care. No massive upheaval ensued, but it marked the start of a long and steady decline.

Something in me died, and I lost the fire to carry on and fight anymore as the pain flared up before fading away. I kept sinking into the depths before resurfacing, but this constant drowning resulted in an inability to keep my head above water. My son had died, my daughter did not want to know me, my marriage had fallen apart, and I was involved in a relationship that could go no further. I had spent years progressing my career and turning our house into a home, but everything I held dear and important no longer mattered. I felt no anger, no bitterness; just an intense nothing.

I reached the point where I began experiencing suicidal thoughts. These feelings of desperation and complete desolation occurred many times, but I had lost my way travelling too far along that bleak road to consider seeking help. I had nothing to live for and my loss engulfed everything around me. Taking your own life is easier said than done and required a courage I lacked. I considered the slitting of my wrists too gruesome a prospect, and an overdose may be unsuccessful, leaving me crippled. A firearm would have been ideal, but the UK is a gun free society.

The prospect of the aftermath countered these deadly serious thoughts. Sara and my mother were grief stricken by Max's death, and others followed close behind. Committing suicide might be another turn of the ratchet, and I was unsure if they could survive further loss. Many people suffered considerably after he died, and I desperately felt this should go no further. I had visions that my suicide might trigger ever-expanding ripples, and the desire to build something positive from Max's death eventually outweighed the need to end my suffering. My self-destructive thoughts eased. When they returned, they were transitory, and I just needed to start anew tomorrow.

Cancer Echoes

Chapter 17

Paula, Sara, and I were haunted by cancer echoes because we had symptoms raising the suspicion we too might have developed the disease. We had lived through false alarms and were aware of the pitfalls. One plausible explanation is that these were psychological reactions to Max's death, but the blood and physical evidence of swellings suggested otherwise. Paula and Sara needed hospital tests, and even with hindsight these symptoms would raise the same concerns.

The first suspicion of cancer occurred with Paula while Sara was nursing Max in the Royal Marsden during his transplant. I had put Paula to bed and was watching television when I heard her crying. I rushed upstairs to her bedroom but could not find her anywhere. Despite calling her, she did not reply, and I slipped into a blind panic. I eventually found her lying extremely upset on the floor next to our bed. Thinking I was sleeping, she could not understand my failure to come to her aid. Paula was crying and coughing badly, and I calmed her, but the hacking continued. As we cuddled, she projectile vomited over me and the carpet. I then became really rattled when she began vomiting mucus. Sara and I cleared up Max's sick daily, changed his bed and cleaned him, and if you needed help, then you called a nurse who fetched fresh sheets. I tried as best as possible to clean the mess, but Paula wanted me constantly by her side. I rang Sara, who drove back at once, and we cleaned the room and comforted our unwell daughter. Having made the call, I realised I probably could have coped. You steel yourself to the rigours of living at the hospital, but this situation caught me unawares, at home, with a different child and no one to help.

Paula's persistent stomach-ache raised the spectre of a further cancer. Sara and I tried persuading ourselves another case was too unlikely, but we had been down that path before. When the consultant delivered Max's second diagnosis, he said, "This is rare." Sara retorted, "Don't talk to us about rare; we know rare." We no longer had any confidence in the scarcity of childhood cancer because experience had taught us otherwise. Sara thought Lymphoma began with coughs and so we took Paula to the doctor, who assuaged our fears and diagnosed a viral infection.

After the revelation that Max might be cancer prone, our consultant discussed our family history of cancer. These questions were probing for hereditary implications of his disease. She told us the Marsden could test for an abnormality in the p53 tumour suppression gene, which prevents uncontrolled multiplication of cells. If faulty, then removal of this one of many brakes for runaway cell growth can lead to cancer. Despite the test potentially explaining Max's multiple illnesses, she said the hospital had no intention of testing him. This shocked me because the question "Why my child?" is an unanswerable demand made by every parent to their consultant. She had told us a potential resolution, and in the same breath denied us the opportunity of answering this question. This anomaly was explained with care.

"Let me outline the medical, ethical, and practical consequences of carrying out a p53 test, because the results have knock-on effects that you may not have considered.

"A positive p53 result indicates a gene defect, but you and we would be no better off regarding Max's wellbeing. This fact won't change his treatment or improve his chances of survival. It only provides us with a partial insight and would just be another piece in the complex jigsaw puzzle of Max's cancers. It's just information that might satisfy your curiosity.

"A treatment targeting this gene would be a different matter. This may arise in the next ten years given the rapid advances in genetics, but at present there's none and thus no gain from performing the test. This is my view as a doctor treating your child.

"However, a positive test has further repercussions. In this scenario there's a chance you as parents might carry the same defective gene and theoretically have a higher chance of developing cancer before reaching older age. This is only likelihood, and not a certainty. What can be gained from that knowledge? An immediate and natural reaction to a positive test result for Max is a request by both of you for the procedure. If either of you then tested positive, you may view the results as a potential death sentence. Despite the lack of material changes in your outlook, this might severely damage your lives, and to what purpose?

"Although you have been coping with your lives without these facts, this may change based on the test results. You may think it stops there; it doesn't. Even if you can countenance this knowledge, then the next question is Paula's welfare. If one of you proved positive for the p53 mutation, that may well suggest a 50% possibility she might have inherited this flaw. Yet again, requesting a test for Paula would be a human reaction. Let's say one of you proves positive, and she tests positive too; where's the benefit? None exists and there could be significant misery for everyone.

"That suffering would be based on a suspected predisposition to cancer, but we cannot quantify that risk. At present you've tremendous burdens dealing with Max's rare and extreme condition, and further stress is not something I recommend."

This was sobering. She had plunged us into complexities we could never have imagined.

"If Max proved positive, could you test Paula without testing us?"

"No, we'd have to prove the link back to you as parents to justify testing her. But there's more. I've discussed the medical and ethical implications of performing the test, but there are other very practical reasons for not pursuing this investigation. A positive test may create issues for any insurance, because the law obliges you to tell insurers of material facts affecting your policies. A p53 gene mutation falls into this category and might invalidate your life insurance. Your mortgage may become invalid because there's no guarantee you'll survive and meet the commitment to the loan. A fact that helps no one may lead to the breakdown of your family and loss of your home. I must stress again that a positive result is just information, because we don't know the precise consequences of a defective p53 gene in cancer development. If any of you tested positive and did not develop cancer, this would highlight the pointlessness of this knowledge."

Initially we chose not to send Max's blood for testing, but afterwards rescinded our decision.

"Sara and I discussed the p53 test and decided not to proceed based on what you told us, but we have an alternative suggestion."

"What do you have in mind?"

"We've taken on board everything you said and understand your recommendation not to go ahead with the test. However, we're in a precarious position with Max and very aware of the slim chances of his survival. We want to do as much as possible towards helping other children in his position. Given the rareness of Max's condition, we strongly feel you should investigate any information which might help more families. It might improve your understanding of the processes leading to multiple cancers. If true, then could you perform the test but not inform us of the outcome? On that basis, we'll never need to declare anything to the insurance companies because we don't know the result."

She looked at us curiously. "Yes, that may well be possible. Whether or not this is the case, thank you for thinking of the other children."

"As parents confronting childhood cancer, we feel helpless, but this could make a small difference. It would mean a lot to us; will you test Max?"

"I'm afraid that decision is not up to me, but I'll submit your request to the Ethics Committee and let you know their reply."

The hospital performed the test and withheld the result. Despite this, the door was always open, and the outcome was available should we ever change our minds. That seemed to be that. But not quite because the test resulted in unforeseen repercussions when comments made by consultants convinced me it had been positive. I thought we were living with a hidden demon but was unsure how it affected us.

After Max died, we lived with the possibility of his cancer being hereditary. Genetic defects cause every cancer, but we now faced the prospect of this spectre reaching out from the grave and claiming one of us. Damage can arise from three scenarios, the first being an external influence on the genes of a growing child. Despite being born healthy, some environmental factor led to a cancer-causing mutation. Alternatively, a damaging gene modification in either the father's sperm or the mother's egg can cause childhood cancer, again triggered by the external environment. In the third case an inherent abnormality is present in one or both parents and leads the child to inherit a susceptibility to cancer. This might be due to a specific combination of the parent's genes, or because either the mother or father is also vulnerable to the disease. P53 mutations fall into this latter category, and Sara, Paula, and I could have a predisposition to the disease in this scenario.

In Paula's case we tried balancing hysteria with rational thought, and although another cancer seemed nonsensical, instinct told us otherwise. A fine line exists between "it can't happen twice" and the fact we had seen it before. We ignored her non-specific tiredness and aches and pains but remained vigilant.

After Sara and I separated, I returned one day tired from a business trip in Germany and received an urgent message to call her back. Bursting into floods of tears when I rang, she told me her suspicion that Paula might have Rhabdo. I trusted Sara's judgement and she had shown an acute awareness of Max's condition long before anyone else thought he had a second cancer. Her instincts were as good as the best and she was not prone to rash judgements. Paula had visible and physical symptoms Sara could not ignore, so she had gone via the normal medical channels and consulted an unfamiliar local doctor. He was brusque, arrogant, and unhelpful, even though she explained our family history. Despite assuring her Paula was well, his failure to explain the symptoms left Sara distraught.

Sara was beside herself with worry and aggravated by not being able to contact me. I returned to comfort her and make decisions. Many thoughts came flooding back. A close connection exists between familial Rhabdomyosarcoma and maternal breast cancer. Were my worst and unspoken nightmares materialising; was this an occasion where cancer decimates the family? It happens. I examined Paula and her symptoms alarmed me, but I did not know how to make a judgement. I was treading an invisible tightrope. If Max's p53 test had been positive, then we would not have hesitated getting an instant referral for her at the Royal Marsden. I rang the hospital to get the result; Max had not suffered from a faulty p53 gene.

Sara arranged an appointment for Paula at the local hospital. Before the session began, I drew the doctor aside to explain our concerns and the potential impact of Max's cancers. After noting my worries, he offered to refer her to the Marsden. We declined and said any explanation for the symptoms would comfort us. After the check-up, he gave us the vindication we desperately needed.

Phoenix

Chapter 18

ooking back over the previous years was strange and yet illuminating, because confusing events were caught in the swirling mists. This fog concealed disjointed incidents that only made sense within their own context, because each commanded my immediate attention. I had no continuity or real comprehension of what had occurred throughout those grim times. These mists started to clear during my bereavement counselling, which allowed me to begin to grasp the significance of these experiences. Horrified, I began coming to terms with Max's illnesses, but did not realise my glimpses of the past also required a reckoning with those that followed.

My reconciliation started with the writing of this book, which brought gentle breezes that blew away the cobwebs and haze which had obscured the reality of Max's illness and death. During my bereavement I examined our lives in minute detail and began to come to terms with what had happened. I understood how far I had fallen, and the climb required to re-join the normal world. The closer I looked at the abyss walls, the more I realised there was an exit, and I found toeholds that enabled the long climb back. A thin pinhole of light replaced the darkness that had been my constant companion for two years.

I made resolutions that became my little landmarks during this return journey. Sometimes a few stones dislodged and fell, but that is often the case in life. The prime concern that year was to make headway in my recovery. Although the climb back was difficult, once it started then I knew Max's death was survivable. More than anything else, bereavement needs time; there is no schedule. Time is a powerful mistress and can smooth the hard edges of trauma until events are no longer recognisable. Life starts returning to normal, but this vital period varies from person to person.

Although I suffered from post-traumatic stress and clinical depression during my bereavement, there were few thoughts about when it would end or ever become bearable. What helped me climb back and what stopped me from doing so earlier? Neither of these questions is easy to answer, and professional counsellors might question my actions. I did what was intuitive throughout Max's illnesses because I had no model or training, and we all felt our way. It served me well and I did the same during my grief. No prescriptive solution exists for bereavement because each of us has different beliefs, cultures, and needs. What helps one person may be useless for another. This is a natural process requiring patience, determination, and lots and lots of time.

Should Sara and I have separated so soon after Max died? Probably not, but we both needed to reconcile ourselves with his death. I cared for nothing anymore, had lost everything and was looking for a fresh start, which one can achieve but should not take lightly. I swept my earlier life into oblivion after leaving my home and family, though I did not stop working because we needed an income. This was fortunate, because it is questionable whether I could have survived a complete break from my former existence.

Watching the progress of another child's cancer did not help during my bereavement. This sudden random arrow was harmful to the healing process and added to my depression.

Another factor unhelpful towards recovery was my sinking deeper and deeper into a pool of alcohol. Many nights I sat alone at home and drank, which helped numb the pain and the ever-increasing loneliness creeping up on me. I knew it was happening but just kidded myself that it did not matter. Although I drank to blank out my hurt, it helped neither my self-esteem nor my depression.

A vital feature in my recovery was my resolve to obtain something meaningful from Max's death. Despite being negative at work during my grief, the project resulting from my promise to him had positive aims.

Paula's rapport with me at the time of Max's death varied from non-existent to hostile. However, we began to enjoy each other's company and looked forward to our time together. This growing bond helped me escape my pit of despair.

Prior to Max's illness I had kept fit but abandoned this after his diagnosis. Following his death, I realised I needed to get back into shape to help cope with the emotional battle raging inside me. Not as physically capable as before, I became run down and ill far more often. I tried running but kept injuring myself, so swam as an alternative and found it invigorating.

Another major step forward in my recuperation was a holiday I took in Malaysia two years after Max died. This break from my work routine was an impulsive decision with no expectations. I enjoyed the vacation and had not realised the advantage of living closely with people unaware of his death. While in an Asian jungle on a South China Sea island, I started losing my incessant preoccupation with my loss of Max. There was no revelation, no miraculous resolution, but the uphill climb began. Sometimes it faltered, but otherwise I made steady progress towards resuming a normal life.

One more aspect in my recovery was taking time off work. I handed in my notice with no prospective job, and intended visiting friends, starting this book, attending training courses, and taking up parachuting. However, the book dominated most of my time before I received a job offer two months afterwards.

I started writing a diary after Max's second diagnosis to express emotions having no other outlet. Later I discovered that other trauma sufferers recommended a journal for similar reasons. Although the diary served its purpose well by voicing my immediate feelings, "Memories of Max" resulted in a detailed examination of events occurring over the previous six years. This painful process required the revisiting of every emotion, but the recounting of this period in my life led to me accepting its reality. Writing entails examining content, grammar, and sentence structure. This constant rereading leads to a progressive desensitisation. Revisiting so many of those difficult days had a numbing effect, where the horrific became the familiar, and suffering converted to experience. The subjective became objective, and I ceased being an actor as I slipped into the role of an observer. Events still caused tears each time I read them, but gradually the distress receded. Cathartic, the book drew a line under Max's sickness and death.

Should I have sought further help in coping with my bereavement? In retrospect, this would have been beneficial. Why did I not do this? I had briefly tried talking openly to friends and relations, but I could not express my surfacing feelings, and they could not even vaguely understand what I managed to articulate. Few could offer the consolation required, and I became convinced that I needed to cope with Max's death alone. Looking back, professional support would have helped me avoid much suffering. Hindsight is helpful, but impossible when you are alone within the eye of a storm. My life had become so introspective and lacked objectivity. I recommend anyone in comparable circumstances seeks specialised support.

Parachuting had always been on my bucket list, and I had a niggling thought I was making excuses for not achieving my goals. If only I had the time; if only it was not so expensive. I worried I was becoming an armchair dreamer and was reluctant to look back ten years' hence and regret grasping at opportunities. My first jump, strapped to an instructor, involved plummeting one mile in thirty seconds and sinking the rest gracefully by parachute. It was so exhilarating that I took up the sport. Unexpectedly calm in the plane prior to my solo jump, the adrenaline coursed during the slow-motion moment when I threw myself into empty space. This is truly letting go, and you fall into the void with enormous faith. After managing a few jumps, I shelved this activity because of the lengthy periods devoted to sitting round waiting for the right weather conditions. I had also begun lots of other projects and realised I would not finish them with barely any free time.

The important aspect of the parachuting was my can-do attitude, and little else was more daunting than finding the courage to jump out of a plane. I experienced a tremendous sense of achievement in meeting this small milestone, which gave me the impetus to continue with the book and other projects.

Bereavement also includes letting go, which involves grieving, accepting, and then finally reconciling yourself with the death of a loved one. It was my perception that the solution to grief solely required ultimate acceptance of your loss. I had done this and did not believe Max had passed into another dimension or existence. This recognition helped because some take years to even accept their child's death. Grieving, however, is a complex sieving process, where you leave the worst of the past behind you and keep the best as tender loving memories.

The constant setbacks while nursing Max had eroded my confidence, but this was gradually rediscovered. I began believing in myself again and took risks I would never have taken beforehand, which resulted in success I could not have imagined when he died. My recovery started. There were still black empty days of despair when tired or stressed and the emotions came flooding back, but they were few and far between. The pain hid quietly behind a curtain, like a body propped up at an Irish wake and swathed in a shroud. Now and then the covering slips and the figure grimaces, giving a rictus smile leaving everyone shaken to the core, but they soon forget, and the celebration continues. It is necessary to endure the pain before it fades peacefully into the past. I knew I just had to move beyond those days and that these emotions would be short-lived.

The bereaved often fear that letting go fails to preserve the memories of the child in their mind's eye. You do not want to relinquish those recollections but expect to crystallise those times in amber as a museum of moments. But one must work through the grief to release its intensity. This is not a conscious move but is time and nature slowly stitching the wounds. Letting go does not mean you do not care; it means you adjust and look forward instead of back into the past. This does not involve forgetting, but instead remembering with fondness and care, not anguish and pain. It signifies a movement beyond this terrible past, and into something new.

Was I bitter? Yes, sometimes when I looked back at the period lost to Max's cancers and asked, "Why?" Six years beforehand we had woken and been handed an open-ended prison sentence. There had been no trial, no formal judgement, and no one provided reasons or said how long it would last.

I needed to contribute meaningfully to mitigate this tragic mess. I could not repay the phenomenal kindness and care shown by others, but I reached a stage where I had the strength to help people again. Subsequently, I spent twelve years volunteering for Samaritans, the listening service for the suicidal and those in despair. This was my way of giving something back for the support we had received throughout Max's illnesses.

Grief is intensely personal, and its resolution needs to come from within. Friends, relations, and counsellors can help. But at the end of the day the desire and determination to move forward are also required.

I learned much about life and myself by living through Max's cancers and death. I spent a long time reconciling myself with them, but eventually discovered his strength and willpower. We cannot change the past, but we can mould our future. One way of resolving a death is by setting little goals and doing everything to reach them. When you achieve your aims, then pat yourself on the back and set another. If you do not reach a target, put it down to experience and formulate other ambitions. We only live once and cannot rewrite parts of life's script which did not work. A bright and vital light shines at the end of the tunnel. Reach for it.

In his last year I did not regard Max as my son, but as an equal and my best friend. Sara and I were very honest with him and he rewarded us with an exceptional mutual trust, confidence, and love. We went through tough times coping with his cancers and are honoured and immensely proud to have had him as our child.

These are my memories of Max.

Afterword

While writing this deeply personal book, I questioned the relevance of my experiences to the world at large, and whether it should be published. I had read two books that put my emotions to shame: Brian Keenan's "An Evil Cradling" and "The Railwayman" by Eric Lomax. Both these men suffered in a manner way beyond my comprehension, and my journey was a mere afterthought compared to the abominations they endured. After much deliberation, I decided I still had a story to tell. It is a valid account giving readers insight to daily events for lots of families, and of which most people are ignorant. I hope this raises more public awareness for them and others with similar experiences.

The preceding chapters, written in 1999, suggest that I had recovered from Max's death at the time of writing. But on later reflection I think it took eight years before I could say that I was leading any form of normal life. Again, events often look very different when viewed with hindsight.

"Memories of Max" had a somewhat extended 22-year gestation before publication. I completed the first draft in late 1999, before seeking criticism and advice from Alice Thomas Ellis: a distant relation, editor, and Booker Prize nominee. I met her later the following year, and to my surprise she described the book as "not just moving, but very impressive." She put me in touch with Duckworth, the publishing house she had owned and run with her husband.

My meeting with the publisher was not fruitful, so I created a website for the book in early 2000 but was unsure of my audience. Bereaved parents struck me as an implausible readership because of the unlikelihood of them wanting to read about the loss of a child. Likewise, those with afflicted children undergoing treatment would be trying to manage their existing burdens. The Guestbook feedback from these families surprised me. They found solace and validation in seeing their own emotions and reactions reflected in my writing. The book also moved other readers unconnected with childhood cancer.

Spurred on by the success of the website, I approached a publishing agent who submitted "Memories of Max" to twelve of the top British publishers. One described it as "exceptionally harrowing but at the same time a remarkable feat of narration." Another had to break from reading to ring and check on the wellbeing of his granddaughter. Despite being impressed, none of the publishers were prepared to accept the book, because they believed it was not a commercial proposition due to its content.

In 2012 my provider closed its Web Hosting service and so I removed "Memories of Max" from the Web. I considered self-publishing in 2014, but the work involved was too time consuming. In 2018, two close friends, within a week of one another, suggested I self-publish. The latest version of Amazon's Kindle made this a realistic proposition, and I wanted to draw a line under this project. I did a comprehensive re-edit with Paula's help, which resulted in a 30% reduction in the original manuscript, which I eventually published in August 2020.

The Wolfson Children's Cancer Unit as described in this book was radically revamped, courtesy of a £16 million donation. The Duke of Cambridge opened the renamed Oak Centre for Children and Young People in 2011.

In early 2020, a report recommended the consolidation of children's cancer services in central London on a single site, because the Royal Marsden does not have a paediatric intensive care unit (PICU). Instead, it uses the services of Saint Georges Hospital, 8 miles away. The threatened closure provoked outrage by existing and former families linked to the Unit. It resulted in a petition to the Government to retain the Oak Centre and was signed by over 35,000 people. The Covid-19 crisis resulted in delays to the review, and the outcome was still not clear when "Memories of Max" was published.

I read the relevant reports (NCAT review of 2011 and the London Paediatric Oncology Review of 2015) and understood their concern but felt that they had not taken into account several issues. The following primary considerations appear to have been ignored.

The current Oak Centre is easy to reach because of its proximity to the M25 motorway. Taking a neutropenic child into central London increases the risk of complications and creates even more stress for parents who are only just coping, especially if they need to use public transport. There is also the inevitable loss of the benefits of having clinical treatment and research currently performed at Sutton. This site is also earmarked for the London Cancer Hub, leading to a potential even greater loss of benefits, but this development was not foreseen at the time the original reports were written.

The proposed relocation of the Unit does not appear to have factored in the overwhelming support of its service users. Despite the lack of a PICU, there is massive love and loyalty for the Unit by the families that use it, and this was also true in 1997. This support derives both from families who have lost a child as well as those whose child has survived. I sincerely hope that an alternative solution is found, because dismantling the current service is foolhardy and almost criminal.

If you want to feedback comments, please use the Customer Review button on the relevant Amazon page for "Memories of Max." I can be contacted via the following email address, but I cannot guarantee I will reply to every email – allanbuchanan23@gmail.com

If you have a child with cancer, please do not view Max's case as typical because treatments change and vary compared to those described back in 1993. Our circumstances of multiple cancers were exceptional, although many of the emotions are not. I send you my love and my thoughts are with you.

Allan Buchanan – August 2020.

Acknowledgements

have acknowledged many people and organisations but want to express my gratitude again.

The Royal Marsden Children's Unit: The praise for the staff throughout this book is inadequate and no words could ever truly express my thanks to them. I am grateful for their love, skill, and dedication.

The Royal Marsden Auxiliary Departments: These include the MRI, Radiography, X-ray, Ultrasound, and other units involved in childhood cancer treatment. These staff always made a special effort for the children and did everything possible to fit them into tight schedules. Nurses, doctors, and technicians worked through their lunch breaks or stayed after hours to do a sudden vital test. Thank you.

Our local doctor, and the Royal Marsden Support Team: Each of you had a demanding task caring for us and Max in his last days at home. You performed it with a compassionate and unintrusive empathy, and we could have asked for no more.

Kara: You did not nurse the patient; you nursed our family. We are thankful for your exceptional love and care.

Rainbow Trust: You provided respite and support for terminal children and their families. We deeply valued your help.

Make-A-Wish Foundation: You gave us a much remembered and necessary holiday. Your open days were an excellent time out for the family, and it was wonderful meeting and seeing old friends.

Saint John's School Cancer Fund: Thank you for your fund raising and our break in Hastings.

Electronic Data Systems: You showed a sensitivity and commitment most parents do not see from their employers. I cannot thank you enough for the time you gave me with Max.

Sara: Thank you for being such an excellent mum to Max.

Sara's and my family: Thanks for your unending support throughout the illnesses, during Max's last days, and in the turmoil that followed.

To those who suggested help which we did not accept: We appreciated your considerate offers, but we wanted to do things our own way.

After the first transcript, I asked several people for constructive criticism. The "Auntie Review" included my sisters, sisters-in-law, and close friends. Many thanks for your time and feedback.

Paula: She has had a difficult life having lost her brother and suffered from major mental and physical health problems. Her determination and success in overcoming these issues was inspiring. Paula helped me edit the book and highlighted many errors and I am thankful for her criticism, which significantly shaped the eventual manuscript.

Special thanks go to the late Alice Thomas Ellis. She reviewed the book, which was a very painful process given that she had lost two children, and I would not have continued without her support.

Medical Glossary

Acute Myeloid Leukaemia (AML)	An aggressive blood cancer in the bone marrow.
	Acute: Rapid and aggressive. Myeloid: Related to bone marrow. Leukaemia: Cancer of blood forming tissue.
Bone Marrow Transplant	A procedure that replaces damaged or faulty bone marrow with healthy cells. Bone marrow is the soft, fatty tissue inside your bones, which produces blood cells.
Chemotherapy	Chemotherapy is the use of drugs to destroy cancer cells because it prevents them from growing and dividing. It has more of an effect because they usually grow and divide faster than normal cells.
Cheyne–Stokes Breathing	An abnormal pattern of breathing commonly seen before death. Periods of shallow breath alternate with deeper and rapid breaths, which may be followed by a pause before starting again and can become noisy because

of the build-up of mucus.

E. Coli	Escherichia coli is a type of bacteria that normally lives in your intestines and is also found in the gut of some animals. Most types of E. coli are harmless and even help keep your digestive tract healthy, but some strains can cause diarrhea if you eat contaminated food.
Fentanyl	A strong opioid painkiller used as an anaesthetic and to treat severe pain. It is also illegally used as a recreational drug, and in 2016 was the most common cause of overdose deaths in the United States.
First-line Antibiotics	First-line drugs are first administered for diseases. They are usually chosen due to less side effects and high clinical effectiveness.
Graft Versus Host Disease (GVHD)	A potentially serious complication during stem cell transplants involving donor cells. The donor's cells (the Graft) view the patient's healthy cells (the Host) as foreign, and attack and damage them.
Granulocyte Colony Stimulating Factor (GCSF)	A growth factor that stimulates the bone marrow to produce granulocytes (a type of white blood cell) and stem cells and release them into the bloodstream.
Hickman Line	A small long tube that is placed into a vein in the chest and ends in a larger vein just above the heart. It is used for long-term access to the veins and can be used to give

chemotherapy, intravenous medications, nutrition, and to draw blood.

Immunosuppression	The suppression of the body's innate ability to ward off disease and infection. It may be the result of a disease that targets the immune system, or as a consequence of pharmaceutical agents used to fight certain conditions, like cancer.
Magnetic Resonance Imaging (MRI)	A non-invasive imaging technology that produces three dimensional detailed anatomical images. It is used for disease detection, diagnosis, and treatment monitoring.
Meningitis	An infection of the protective membranes that surround the brain and spinal cord, which can cause blood poisoning and result in permanent damage to the brain or nerves.
Methicillin Resistant Staphylococcus Aureus (MRSA)	An infection caused by Staphylococcus bacteria, which is resistant to many different antibiotics. These bacteria naturally live in the nose and on the skin and generally do not cause any harm. Also known as "Golden Staph".
Neutropenic/ Neutrophil	Neutropenia occurs when a person has a low level of neutrophils, which are a type of white blood cell. Neutrophils are made in the bone marrow and fight infection by destroying harmful bacteria and fungi (yeast) that invade the body.

P53 Gene	A protein also known as the Guardian of the Genome and which is a tumour suppression gene. If a person inherits only one functional copy of the p53 gene from their parents, they are predisposed to cancer and usually develop several independent tumours in a variety of tissues in early adulthood.
Paediatric Intensive Care Unit (PICU)	An area within a hospital specialising in the care of critically ill infants, children, teenagers, and young adults.
Palliative Treatment	An interdisciplinary medical caregiving approach aimed at optimising quality of life and mitigating suffering among people with serious and complex illnesses.
Platelets	A component of blood that reacts to bleeding from blood vessel injury by clumping, thereby initiating a blood clot.
Post-Traumatic Stress Disorder (PTSD)	A mental disorder that can develop after someone is exposed to a traumatic event or threats to a person's life. Symptoms include disturbing thoughts and feelings, mental or physical distress, an increase in the fight-or-flight response, and amnesia. PTSD sufferers often experience nightmares, intrusive and recurrent recollections, as well as dissociative episodes which are also known as flashbacks.
Registrar	The registrar is the ward's senior doctor and is usually contactable on site, as opposed to the senior consultant, who attends ward rounds and meetings at specific times.

Relapse

The reoccurrence of a previous cancer.

Remission

Complete remission indicates that the signs and symptoms of cancer have disappeared in response to treatment.

Rhabdomyosarcoma (RMS)

An aggressive and highly malignant soft tissue cancer, referred to as "Rhabdo" in the Unit.

Rhabdo: Rod-like.
Myo: Muscle.
Sarcoma: Tumour.

Salmonella

A common bacterial disease that affects the intestinal tract. Salmonella bacteria typically live in animal and human intestines and are shed through faeces. Humans become infected most frequently through contaminated water or food.

Septicaemia

A term used to describe blood poisoning caused by bacteria entering the bloodstream, which is potentially life-threatening.

Tumour

A swelling of a part of the body, generally without inflammation, caused by an abnormal growth of tissue, which can be benign or malignant.

Warfarin

A medication used as an anticoagulant to treat blood clots. Also used as rat poison.

Printed in Great Britain
by Amazon